CONTEMPORARY ITALIAN POETRY

An Anthology

Contemporary Italian Poetry

AN ANTHOLOGY

EDITED BY CARLO L. GOLINO

UNIVERSITY OF CALIFORNIA PRESS
BERKELEY AND LOS ANGELES 1962

To A. J.

UNIVERSITY OF CALIFORNIA PRESS
BERKELEY AND LOS ANGELES

CAMBRIDGE UNIVERSITY PRESS
LONDON, ENGLAND

© 1962 BY THE REGENTS OF THE UNIVERSITY OF CALIFORNIA

LIBRARY OF CONGRESS CATALOG CARD NO. 62-7436

DESIGNED BY ADRIAN WILSON

FOREWORD

This anthology is the first methodical presentation of its kind which has been attempted for the English-speaking reader. The work, which is not conceived historically, but which nonetheless embraces the main literary movements of our age, is an act of good will on the part of Carlo L. Golino, a tireless reader and student of Italian poetry. It is no less a sign of his faith in the American observer of the phenomena of European art in all its manifestations—a faith expressed in a time become arid from ideological differences and opposing political orientations such as almost deny the possibilities of creative intelligence to the man of our century. Fortunately, it is not my duty to reconstruct here a critical panorama (a most difficult task even now when one would expect the twentieth century might be viewed objectively). Instead, my purpose is to invite the American reader to acquaint himself with a poetry which, until now, has appeared, without any conscious intention of its own, as an elaboration of the poetics of European symbolism and decadentism. Might it be that the form of this poetry is such that it is not susceptible of analysis, that it has no independent life apart from the tradition? The patient English-speaking reader will immediately notice that the truth is quite the contrary. Carlo L. Golino, who is also the faithful translator of most of these poems, has evolved a "classification" by which he groups the poets according to their characteristics and relates them to the various cultural currents. As every anthology reveals its editor, so the present collection and arrangement display Golino's critical taste, his predilection for certain subject matter, his prudence in choosing poets of the new generation.

I must add only that the most notable names of contemporary Italian poetry are included in this anthology (one might wish to add two or three names at the very most), with or without their private histories as they were decided within the human time span of two wars that have altered the very nature of feeling and the ability of these *resistenti* of literature to continue to speak in verse.

Salvatore Quasimodo

Milan, June 1961

PREFACE

The most important development in the history of Italian poetry of the twentieth century has been the emergence and the acceptance of what has been termed "hermetic poetry." It is around this school and its chief representatives that we find the essential elements, the nourishing matter of new poetical trends; and its tenets have been accepted, at least in part, by even its most bitter opponents. In fact, the prolonged dispute between "hermetics" and "anti-hermetics" is the best and clearest evidence of how irrevocably "hermeticism" has gnawed away at the traditional canons of Italian poetry.

The term *poesia ermetica* was used for the first time by Francesco Flora as the title of a volume he published in 1936 as an appraisal of current poetry. Actually, by 1936 the intensity of feeling and the polemical spirit of the dispute was diminishing, and hermetic poetry was an accomplished fact even though a name for it was just being coined. Since 1936, Italian poetry has followed a varied and difficult course, but the hermetic experience has remained its fundamental point of reference.

A second and equally important characteristic of Italian poetry in this century has been its emergence from local and national boundaries and its appearance as part of European literary currents. It has been said that Italian literature of today, and poetry in particular, is European in content and character, and Italian in language. One may not wish to subscribe fully to this statement, but it is beyond doubt that Italian writers and poets of this period, unlike their counterparts of the previous generation, share their problems and orientation with their colleagues in other European countries. This emergence as a European literature has implied a new attitude toward national traditions, but these traditions have never been abandoned and they still remain the key to modern Italian poetry.

As the twentieth century opened, Italian poetry was dominated by Carducci, Pascoli, and D'Annunzio; a mighty triad whose influence had to be overcome if there was to be something new. All three poets had their roots in the Romantic movement, but their individual developments varied appreciably. Carducci represented a reaction and used his antiromantic rhetorical eloquence to endow poetry with a historical and civic function. But in his more intimate poems eloquence was subdued. Here Carducci showed his romantic heritage and pointed the way to a new technique of poetic expression.

In Pascoli the romantic traits are more evident. The "homey" atmosphere of his poetry, and the naïve, childlike sensitivity to a nature no longer seen from the standpoint of classical harmony were of romantic derivation. The same can be said of Pascoli's language, which he attempted to strip of eloquence and to simplify—or at least he appeared to do so. Actually, he strove laboriously for symbolic suggestiveness. Romantic as well was Pascoli's restlessness and insecurity; his tendency toward the morbid and his insistence on his sufferings—feelings that he was never able to lift to the level of tragic sentiments.

D'Annunzio represents the final, exasperated phase of romanticism; but his influence lasted longer than that of the others, since he did not die until 1937 (Carducci died in 1907; Pascoli in 1912). Decadent poet, interpreter of febrile sensualism, self-appointed superman—D'Annunzio has none of Carducci's civic wrath. His is the furor of the self-possessed man in search of refined sensations, a search justified in the name of a superhuman morality and esthetics. Pascoli's melancholy and subdued morbidity is turned by D'Annunzio into a willful adventure into the abnormal, controlled always by a lucid intelligence. It is difficult even today to say what will survive of D'Annunzio's copious writings, but his linguistic power has had a great, though often negative, influence on later poets. Had D'Annunzio not made his search for the sonorous and evocative word, the subsequent renewal of Italian poetry could not have taken place. Nor can we understand the intentional poverty of language of the later *crepuscolari*, or the hermetics' return to the pristine meaning of words, unless we understand that these are reactions against D'Annunzio's baroque opulence.

As the new century began, D'Annunzio seemed already cast in the role of bête-noire for all would-be reformers of Italian poetry. The crepuscolari ("twilight poets")—a group so named by G. A. Borgese—were the first poets to oppose him. Its chief exponents were Guido Gozzano and Sergio Corazzini, both of whom died young and infused into their poetry a sense of impending death. "Twilight" aptly describes the quality of their technique and expression. The twilight poet, conceiving himself as powerless before the inevitable, sings in a subdued voice. His languid resignation is counterbalanced only by a mildly ironic self-examination which assigns the poet an even more humble and passive role. These poets do not face death with dreams of unachieved glory, or with unsatisfied appetites; revolt, struggle, and violence are absent. They are deliberate anti-intellectuals, and their themes are drawn from the tritest and most unrefined objects and situations, from the most bourgeois milieux and customs. Theirs is poetry in a minor key in which the civic fury of Carducci, the childlike naïveté of Pascoli, and D'Annunzio's superhuman efforts dissolve in an inconsolable but gentle irony.

This poetry of self-denial, of meek resignation that hides a deep sense of anguish, is the first novel movement of the century, and though closely bound to its immediate predecessors it marks a break. With the crepuscolari, twentieth-century Italian poetry has really begun.

At approximately the same time that Gozzano and Corazzini were publishing their poetry, a review was founded in Florence, in 1903, by Giovanni Papini and Giuseppe Prezzolini. They were hardly twenty but were burning with desire for an active intellectual life. Their review *Leonardo*, which lived less than five years, was the first successful effort to free Italian culture from its provincial and national restrictions. *Leonardo* did not deny Italian traditions; it wanted instead to integrate these with other cultures, to break away from Italian cultural isolation once and for all. The importance of this review for Italian culture of the period has been widely and justly recognized. The editors, by their own admission, were strongly oriented toward philosophy. However, *Leonardo*'s influence was so far-reaching that it was felt in the realm of the arts and poetry as well. It was *Leonardo*, indeed, that fostered conditions that made the outburst of "futurism" seem a logically inevitable consequence.

Leonardo had advocated a modification of conditions in Italy so as to bring Italian culture to an international level. The futurists now demanded the total destruction of every tradition, national or otherwise; but they had learned their lesson from *Leonardo*. They knew that if their break with the past was to have any effect it could not be carried out in the provincial circles of Italian intellectualism. Hence it was from Paris that they launched their program. The futurist manifesto, which was written in French and published in *Figaro* on February 22, 1909, is undoubtedly one of the most interesting documents of modern Italian culture. Although its consequences were not quite what its formulators had foreseen, it had a long-lasting effect. The manifesto was definite and clear: break with tradition, destroy the past, close all libraries and museums, look to the future and to the future alone. Moonlight has been the source of inspiration for generations of poets, but, announced the futurists, we hereby abolish moonlight and we shall draw inspiration from our own modern times and life, from our inventions, from our machines, from speed—modern man's greatest conquest—from violence, from war; for life is basically a struggle. The general statement of principles was followed by a *manifesto tecnico* for literature and poetry. Poetry for the futurists was to be intuition expressed through analogies that would become more and more complex and remote in their relations. Traditional syntax was to be set aside in favor of a new syntax of *parole in libertà* (free words). Verbs were to be used only in the infinitive; adjectives and adverbs were abolished; punctuation was no longer deemed necessary; and poetic meters were considered an anachronism. What did futurist poetry look like? What was its character? Here is a representative example:

monoplano = balcone–rosa–ruota–tamburrrrrro trapano–tafano > disfatta–araba bue sanguinolenza

macello
        ferite
                rifugio
                            oasi
umidità ventaglio freschezza

monoplane = balcony–rose–wheel–drrrrrum drill–gadfly >
defeat–arab ox bloodiness

butchery
        wounds
                shelter
                          oasis
humidity fan coolness

    This sample, from Filippo Tommaso Marinetti's *Battaglia*, is a brief but clear indication of how drastic a change was implied by futurism if its extreme innovations had prevailed. But this was not to be. Futurism was a movement born out of an understandable desire for new horizons, but it grew from a sterile soil and lacked the substance of either a moral or emotional content. Practically every poet of the period was directly or indirectly connected with the futurist movement at one time or another, yet it would be difficult to classify any single one of them as a futurist. The lone exception was Marinetti, the founder and prophet of futurism; he remained loyal to it throughout its brief life. Nevertheless, futurism rendered a great service to Italian letters. It cleared the air momentarily, by exposing many a moldy and worm-eaten tradition, and it reëmphasized the necessity for Italy's entrance into the current of European culture. It also showed, through its exaggeration and eccentricities of technique, the possibility and the desirability of syntactical and lexical reforms. This lesson was not lost, and it bore fruit later at the hands of true poets.

    Reform was now in the air. Futurism ran its course quickly; but if life was not entirely in the future as it had claimed, a return to the past was also impossible. This was becoming more and more evident not only in relation to the arts and literature but on a moral plane as well. Italian culture, it seemed, had to be integrated in all its manifestations into the life of the nation if it was to have a true significance. A new magazine appeared, a new banner was raised, a new impetus was found. The same Giuseppe Prezzolini who several years before had founded *Leonardo* with Papini now founded *La Voce*. It was 1909, the year of the futurist manifesto. *La Voce* quickly attracted the attention and the support of the best minds of Italy. Prezzolini's first and foremost credo was action—at all times, at all costs—and this rage for action was shared by a great many. The perplexity that followed the collapse of futurism was quickly overcome by the possibilities proclaimed by *La Voce*, and the response was general. Thus, among the *vociani* we find G. Papini, A. Palazzeschi, C. Sbarbaro, P. Jahier, C. Rèbora, and D. Campana, to mention but a few; their names represent a list of the major poets of the time. It would be difficult to speak of a poetics of the vociani, for theirs was a heterogeneous group and the poetical solution that each one of them found for their common problem varied appreciably from one to the other. What united them and gave their movement a certain cohesion was their common desire for a renewed awareness of social and spiritual questions and of moral responsibility. Futurism provided a point of departure and the vociani borrowed freely from it, but added a new kind of dedication. In poetry the results were as varied as the individual solutions to moral problems, but some sort of pattern did emerge in the preference for strongly impressionistic imagery, brief fragmentary compositions, a pervasive use of analogy, and a great freedom in versification.

Let us briefly consider some of the poets of the *Voce* group. Corrado Govoni was still bound to the influence of the crepuscolari; his constant use of analogy to evoke quick impressions was accompanied by the splash of strong colors. Aldo Palazzeschi's poetic vignettes suggested a relationship with the syntactical reforms of the futurists; his experiments with meters and his disregard for punctuation may also be attributable to the same source. The urgency for new moral values never attained any depth in Palazzeschi; it became, rather, a gentle, laconic satire of the middle class, its conventions and its self-satisfaction. Not so in Giovanni Papini, whose satire was often cruel and biting. Papini's unquenchable thirst for knowledge, his ambition, and his bitter sarcasm are the mark of a solitary man searching for a solution within his desolate soul. Only later, when he was reconverted to Catholicism, was he to find peace.

The spiritual vacuum that futurism had left behind is particularly evident in Clemente Rèbora. He best personifies the religious crisis of his generation, which, although it displayed a religious sense, had entertained few religious beliefs. Rèbora's poetry seems to imply that the spiritual aridity of the present is made bearable by an unshakable belief that the future will bring a new Word to fill the vacuum. Failing this belief, we have, as in Camillo Sbarbaro, the disenchanted acceptance of an empty life. For Piero Jahier the moral problem was chiefly one of conscience and principle, and the implied necessity of an open act of faith in them without compromise.

The anguished need for moral self-justification reached a pitch of exasperation in the tragic personality of Dino Campana. None of the poets of *La Voce* achieved the lyric purity of Campana, but his recurring mental derangement, which became permanent in the last part of his short life, precluded any possibility of a personal solution of the problem. The tormented life of Campana found its only relief in outbursts of lyricism, which, when they corresponded to moments of mental lucidity, have no equal in twentieth-century Italian poetry. But more often, his beclouded poetry is only a harmony of words and a race of images. It is nonetheless beautiful, even when it is marred by the obscurities of an infirm mind. Campana roamed over Europe and South America and engaged in the strangest assortment of occupations. He was continually in and out of jails and mental institutions—always poor, alone, urged on only by his devouring anguish. Campana is a modern poet, as are all the other poets of *La Voce*, with whom he shares the credit for having given a sound meaning to the reforms of the futurists and for opening the way to a new life for Italian poetry.

The First World War brought to a climax that sense of moral uneasiness that had characterized the vociani, but it also cut short any further development. After the war Italian poetry moved in two chief currents, one revolving about Giuseppe Ungaretti and the trend that would eventually be termed "hermetic"; the other we shall arbitrarily call "tradition and experiment," for lack of a better term. While it is possible to speak of a hermetic "school" and to define a line of continuity in its exponents, the other current is characterized by the sporadic, often isolated efforts of groups and especially of individuals. For the sake of clarity we shall first examine the current of tradition and experiment, and then turn back to trace the evolution of the hermetic school.

The review *La Ronda*, founded in 1919 by Vincenzo Cardarelli, gave the first impetus toward reëstablishing a basis for Italian letters after the First World War. *La Ronda* proposed a return to tradition, particularly in regard to language. In poetry its ideal model became Leopardi, indicating a desire for the revival of pure lyricism and a return to classicism. In view of the extremist tendencies of the prewar epoch, the *rondisti* decided that Italian as a language was on the brink of dissolution with respect to structure and content; and that the first thing that ought to be done was to "reëducate Italians in the art of writing." This aim, they stated, could only be achieved by a return to the models of such outstanding periods of Italian literature as the late cinquecento, or, in poetry, to Leopardi, whom they considered the most modern among nineteenth-century Italian poets. The desire to reëstablish a historical continuity in the poetical language of Italy, no doubt praiseworthy, was doomed to failure because it ignored the changed times and the new problems they had ushered in. Viewed in retrospect, *La Ronda* now seems a kind of necessary pause—a consolidation of new attitudes—since in spite of their avowed aims, the rondisti had absorbed and exhibited the influence of prewar currents. Only in the poetry of Cardarelli did *La Ronda* produce a significant contribution; otherwise its proposed poetics went unheeded.

Umberto Saba was also a classicist in that he desired to rejuvenate his language at old sources, but there any affinity with the rondisti ends. Although he was one of the most influential figures of Italian twentieth-century poetry, Saba occupied an isolated position throughout his life. Born and raised in Trieste, before the city was reunited to Italy (in 1918 as a result of the First World War), Saba differed in background and development from his contemporaries in Italy. He remained at the edge of Italian culture and his activity seemed always tangential. His poetry issued entirely from his own personality; and his insistence on self-examination gives his work as a whole the appearance of an autobiographical obsession. He foreshadows the hermetics' closed, personal world, and although his language is seldom obscure, he gives certain words an emphatic importance—a habit that suggests the hermetics' technique. The world of Saba recalls the unpretentiousness of the crepuscolari, but there is no resigned meekness in him; indeed, the commonplace world seems brightened by his faith in it.

Other poets outside the prevailing current of hermetic poetry made their appearance between the two world wars. Some who were very young then are still writing today, but their roots are in the twenties and early thirties, and this fact must be kept in mind. Luigi Bartolini was one of the most original poets of the period. Although persecuted by the Fascists he maintained in his poetry an indomitable spirit, a warm human feeling, and an unshakable faith in life. Carlo Betocchi, a "most fervent Catholic," brought to his poetry a profound inner peace, which was reflected in the cheerful moral tone of his verses. Attilio Bertolucci's affectionate personality has given us some of the most refreshing idylls of modern Italian poetry; his graceful verse depicts a tender and gentle nature that is never cloying. In his more recent poetry he has enlarged his horizon, and some of the problems of the modern world have penetrated his intimacy with nature. Sandro Penna, an authentic *petit-maître*, as one critic called him, delicately captures the slightest sensation, the most fleeting impression in poems of epigrammatic brevity. Lastly among these poets we come to Cesare Pavese, one of the most significant writers of modern Italian literature. His tragic death by suicide in 1950 created for years a respectful hesitancy on the part of critics and biographers. But as the veil is lifted it becomes more and more apparent that his writings have been at once a point of arrival and of departure in Italian letters. His poetry, which first appeared in 1936, seemed completely detached from other currents, and for this reason, perhaps, went unnoticed. But Pavese, unlike most of his contemporaries, was acutely aware of the problems of those difficult years. His literary formation had been strongly influenced by English and American literature, and by the Americans in particular, a unique force in prewar Italy—and this seemed to emphasize the non-Italian character of his poetry. In reality Pavese is closely bound to local Piedmontese or Ligurian traditions, and his poetry retains a great deal of the latter's harsh qualities in its difficult and highly intellectual bent. Social and political preoccupations are always present, although he could not be called an *engagé* poet. He was firmly convinced that words must make up the substance and objectivity of poetry; but he also realized that the substantiality of the poetic word (the only real instrument at the disposal of the poet) would never suffice to express his own intimate travail—a vicious circle from which there seemed to be no escape.

The year 1936, when Pavese's first poems appeared, was also the year in which the term *poesia ermetica* made its appearance. Although hermetic poetry was an accomplished fact in this year, to find its roots we must go back to the period immediately following the First World War—the period when Cardarelli and his *La Ronda* group were proposing a return to tradition to give the Italian language new vigor. The efforts of the rondisti were abortive, however, and attention began to be focused on one man, Giuseppe Ungaretti. As Montale stated, Ungaretti was the only one during the war and immediately after who, "alone, in his time, was able to profit by the freedom which was in the air." Born in Egypt of Italian parents, Ungaretti studied at the Sorbonne and during his years in Paris became closely associated with such French men of letters as Apollinaire, Gide, and Valéry. He came to Italy in 1914 and joined the Italian army in 1915 when Italy entered the war. His first collection of poems, *Il porto sepolto*, appeared in 1916, but it was only in 1919 with *L'allegria dei naufraghi* that his poetry began to be noticed. His European education had prepared him to step into the breach that futurism had opened in the solid wall of Italian tradition. His greatest effort, however, was directed toward restoring the poetic "word" to its true meaning and dignity. The crepuscolari, the futurists, and the vociani had an inkling of this necessary reform, but Ungaretti was the first to complete the cycle. For him, "words" could no longer be oratorical, ornamental, pictorial, sensual, or melancholy—words in poetry were to be "subjective and universal," brought to "an extreme state of tension that would fulfill the premise of their meaning." Ungaretti, we might say, was attempting to create a poetry "in progress" in which every word would be restored to its virgin meaning (historically speaking), untainted by the accretions of centuries of conventions, and would thus evoke an immediate, candid image. Upon this premise he began to build his "poetics," enriching it as he went along with a profound emotive content, in which human sorrow allied itself with religious fervor in a language of primitive desperation. There remained the problems of rhythm, of meter, of versification: elements that had reached such a state of chaos that the rondisti had flatly declared that strict verse was dead and buried. Ungaretti, however, remained firm in his faith that Italian poetry could be written with a newly balanced technique; after years of painstaking effort he proved that it could be done. From the earlier works in which the versification seemed almost external to the poetry itself and in which punctuation is almost completely discarded, Ungaretti sought to reconstruct the rhythm of the Italian language by recasting into new form the traditional hendecasyllable. All subsequent Italian poetry felt the impact of this reform.

If Ungaretti was the "creator" of hermetic poetry, it was Eugenio Montale who gave the trend direction and an added dimension. Like Ungaretti, Montale was strongly influenced by a foreign literature. For him, it was English rather than French, particularly through T. S. Eliot, for whom Montale has always felt a close affinity. But Montale's poetic origins can nevertheless be traced to poets of his native Liguria, such as Ceccardo and Sbarbaro, and to a later influence of impressionism. Having accepted Ungaretti's assertion that words must be bared of all ornamentation and brought back to their pristine, evocative meaning, Montale also introduced into his poetry a musicality that is lacking in Ungaretti. "I obeyed a need for musical expression," Montale wrote later. But the divergence between the two men is chiefly philosophical and spiritual. Ungaretti has been defined as the "poet of sorrow"; but his is a human, comprehensible sorrow sustained by a Christian faith. He regards human life as one of suffering but does not preclude the ultimate deliverance from it. Montale is basically a negative spirit. The themes of his poetry revolve around the concept that man is alone and that the world is futile and meaningless. He is a man conscious of his crisis, who lives his crisis from moment to moment, from day to day, to its last bitter instant, without ever being able to overcome it or to leave it behind. It is the crisis of the intellectual and already bears the mark of the later existentialist. In the period between the two world wars, and especially in the years just before the last war, Montale reflects the moral discomfort of a generation that is on its way to utter tragedy and is powerless before it. In poetry the spiritual wasteland of Montale is translated into a detailed depiction of nature—an unfriendly, harsh nature, in which even the spectacle of beauty, of joy, is quickly obscured by the undercurrent of futility that cold reason introduces. Montale's poetry is not easily understandable and requires continuous reflection and effort on the part of the reader, but it possesses a tension, an evocative power, and such novel musical and rhythmical resolutions that it remains unsurpassed in modern Italian literature. The term "hermetic" employed by Francesco Flora to describe the poetry of Ungaretti and Montale was indeed appropriate. It is "hermetic" in its personal and individual character, concentrated inwardly in the poet's effort to resurrect within himself and within the reader the primordial meaning of human existence. The term "hermetic" has often, and incorrectly, been made a synonym of obscurity. The only justification for this common error is that many of those who loudly announced their allegiance to the hermetic school were in fact obscure writers. On the other hand, those who followed in the steps of Ungaretti and Montale and were truly poets gave hermeticism its final brilliant phase, and with Quasimodo in particular it gained a new impetus.

Libero De Libero, Alfonso Gatto, Mario Luzi, and Vittorio Sereni are some of the poets who have contributed greatly to the later hermetic current. De Libero, the poet of Ciociaría (his native land, between Rome and Naples), brings to the austere hermetic technique a refreshing hopefulness and a deep attachment to his land. Alfonso Gatto, a native of Salerno, proves that traditional southern exuberance may be held in check. His "surrealistic idylls," as his compositions have been called, are actually continual attempts to clarify his own moral problems, to discover new forms adaptable to his strongly musical bent. Mario Luzi is, by his own admission, a difficult poet, whose musical verse is heavy with metaphysical thought and a sadness that reveals an inner despair akin to existentialism. Vittorio Sereni echoes the language of the crepuscolari, modified strongly by the influence of Montale. Sereni's poetry is direct, his imagery vivid, and his words chosen carefully so as to create effective symbols.

Salvatore Quasimodo is today the best-known Italian poet outside his country. His Nobel Prize for Literature in 1959 has undoubtedly aided this popularity, but the award was simply a confirmation of his stature. Although Quasimodo's early poetry is closely connected with the hermetic school, he did not arrive at his hermetic experience through a foreign literature, and his roots are strictly in Italian poetry. (If any "foreign influence existed in Quasimodo's formative period it would be the ancient Greek lyric poets, whom he later translated remarkably well into Italian.) And though some of his early poems were even more "difficult" than Montale's, Quasimodo exhibited immediately certain qualities that appealed to a broader and larger audience. No other hermetic poet received so much favor from the public as Quasimodo quickly did in 1942 when he published his volume *Ed è subito sera*. Quasimodo was at the center of the last polemic between hermetics and anti-hermetics. Damned by his enemies and praised by his friends, Quasimodo emerged from this conflict as one of the chief figures of contemporary Italian poetry and the last champion of the hermetic trend. It was at this juncture, soon after the end of the last war, that a marked change appeared in Quasimodo's orientation. Some critics quickly and superficially spoke of a "new Quasimodo," an "anti-hermetic Quasimodo," without realizing that this "second phase" was not a phase at all, but only a logical and imperative development. The war had brought about many new problems, and these were reflected by Quasimodo in a deeper awareness of the modern dilemma. Quasimodo has very clearly defined the function, duties, and objectives of a poet in his *Discorso sulla poesia*, a document that reaffirms the continuity and consistency of all his works. If, as he states in this essay, poetry becomes ethics because it is a representation of beauty, then the poet's responsibility is in direct ratio to his achievement of beauty. In other words, poetry is the expression of a judgment and as such it has a definite effect on the society in which the poet lives; therefore, he cannot separate himself from his particular time and place. These are Quasimodo's basic principles, and he has remained unalterably true to them.

Since the last war, new trends have appeared in Italy. The Italian postwar literature of "neorealism," a tag that appropriate or not seems destined to remain, has had a world-wide diffusion. What about poetry? Can we speak of a neorealist poetry? Yes, but only if we mean by the term a chronological coincidence with the neorealistic trend in narrative literature. Admittedly, postwar poetry does have certain traits in common with neorealism, but to press this parallel could be hazardous. However we wish to describe new trends in postwar Italian poetry, one poet comes immediately to mind: Pier Paolo Pasolini. Pasolini is an *engagé* writer whose themes deal with social and political problems. He is a highly controversial figure in many ways, but the recognition of his poetic vitality has been quick and wide in spite of the strong ideological utterances his work contains. His poetry then is in this sense realistic, and realism of one sort or another seems to be looming heavily on the Italian poetical scene, even when steeped in some of the old themes which Margherita Guidacci treats so beautifully in her poetry.

For a rapid recapitulation of the development of Italian poetry in this century, it might suffice to mention a few milestones: crepuscolari, futurists, vociani, hermetic poetry; and a few names—Gozzano, Campana, Saba, Ungaretti, Montale, Quasimodo. The first half of the century has been an extremely rich period in which Italian poetry has risen to a prominent position in the world, and its strength is far from spent; the second half of the century may bring even greater riches.

* * *

I wish to express my gratitude to the following persons for providing translations and allowing me to include them in this volume: Ronald Farrar, Instructor in Modern Languages at Los Angeles City College, for his translation of Sergio Corazzini; Thomas G. Bergin, Professor of Romance Languages, Yale University, for his translation of Umberto Saba; Cosimo Corsano, Fulbright Research Scholar, Department of Italian, University of California, Los Angeles, for his translation of Vincenzo Cardarelli; Norman T. Di Giovanni, of Boston, Massachusetts, teacher, poet, and translator, for his translation of Cesare Pavese; Lowry Nelson, Jr., Associate Professor of English, University of California, Los Angeles, for his translation of Giuseppe Ungaretti; John A. Scott, Assistant Professor of Italian, University of California, Berkeley, for his translation of Alfonso Gatto; Allen Mandelbaum of Rome, poet and translator, official translator of Salvatore Quasimodo; William F. Weaver of Rome, poet and translator, music critic, for his translation of Pier Paolo Pasolini. I am particularly grateful to Lowry Nelson, Jr., and Cosimo Corsano for their excellent services in attending to many details of revision in my absence from the United States; to Mario Luzi and Roberto Coppini of Florence for their advice and assistance in contacting certain poets; and to Robert Y. Zachary and Geoffrey Ashton of the University of California Press for their patient, competent, and enthusiastic help.

I am indebted and grateful to the following persons and publishing houses for their permission to reproduce and translate the Italian texts contained in this anthology:

Luigi Bartolini for his own poems;
Giulio Einaudi Editore, Turin, and Franz J. Horch Associates, New York, for the poems of Cesare Pavese and Umberto Saba;
Arnoldo Mondadori Editore, Milan, and Farrar, Straus & Cudahy, New York, for the Italian text and the English translations of the poems of Salvatore Quasimodo;
Aldo Garzanti Editore, Milan, for the poems of Sandro Penna and Pier Paolo Pasolini;
Alfonso Gatto for his own poems;
Corrado Govoni for his own poems;
Dottor Renato Gozzano for the poems of Guido Gozzano;
Arnoldo Mondadori Editore, Milan, for the poems of Vincenzo Cardarelli, Libero De Libero, Eugenio Montale, and Giuseppe Ungaretti;
Mrs. Giacinta Papini for the poem of Giovanni Papini;
Dottor Piero Rèbora for the poems of Clemente Rèbora;
Riccardo Ricciardi Editore, Milan–Naples, for the poems of Sergio Corazzini;
Casa Editrice G. C. Sansoni, Florence, for the poems of Attilio Bertolucci and Mario Luzi;
Camillo Sbarbaro for his own poem;
Vanni Scheiwiller Editore, Milan, for the poems of Margherita Guidacci;
Vittorio Sereni for his own poems;
Vallecchi Editore, Florence, for the poems of Carlo Betocchi, Dino Campana, Piero Jahier, and Aldo Palazzeschi.

The specific volumes, and the publisher, from which the individual poems were taken are listed under each poet in "Notes on the Poets."

C. L. G.

Fiesole (Firenze), April, 1961

CONTENTS

Foreword by Salvatore Quasimodo   v
Preface   vii

I TWILIGHT POETS

Guido Gozzano translated by Carlo L. Golino
- La differenza   2
- I colloqui   2
- L'assenza   6

Sergio Corazzini translated by Ronald Farrar
- Desolazione del povero poeta sentimentale   10
- Per organo di Barberia   14

II FUTURISM AND *LA VOCE*

Corrado Govoni translated by Carlo L. Golino
- Paesi   20
- Bellezze   20
- La trombettina   22

Aldo Palazzeschi translated by Carlo L. Golino
- La fontana malata   24
- Ara Mara Amara   28
- Rio Bo   30
- Novembre   30
- Il Palatino   32

Giovanni Papini translated by Carlo L. Golino
- Ottava poesia   34

Clemente Rèbora translated by Carlo L. Golino
- Campana di Lombardia   38
- Dall'immagine tesa   38

PIERO JAHIER   translated by Carlo L. Golino
            Serata 42
CAMILLO SBARBARO   translated by Carlo L. Golino
       Taci, anima stanca di godere 46
DINO CAMPANA   translated by Carlo L. Golino
          Giardino autunnale 48
            La chimera 50
         Viaggio a Montevideo 52
           Donna genovese 54
         Due liriche per S. A. 56
            L'invetriata 56

III   TRADITION AND EXPERIMENT

UMBERTO SABA   translated by Thomas G. Bergin
            La capra 62
          « *Frutta erbaggi* » 62
              Ulisse 64
              Donna 64
           Il vetro rotto 66
           L'arboscello 66
            Felicità 68
             Ceneri 68
VINCENZO CARDARELLI   translated by Cosimo Corsano
             Estiva 72
            Autunno 74
          Adolescente 74
        Sera di Gavinana 78
            Liguria 80
LUIGI BARTOLINI   translated by Carlo L. Golino
        Rima del confino 84
            Colori 84
CARLO BETOCCHI   translated by Carlo L. Golino
          Alla sorella 88
    Un dolce pomeriggio d'inverno 90
CESARE PAVESE   translated by Norman T. Di Giovanni
            Estate 92
       La terra e la morte 92

ATTILIO BERTOLUCCI   translated by Carlo L. Golino
                                                                               Amore   98
                                               La notte d'ottobre   98
                                                             Inverno   100
SANDRO PENNA   translated by Carlo L. Golino
                                     La veneta piazzetta   102
                          I pini solitari lungo il mare   102
                                Il mio amore è furtivo   104
                     La luna di settembre su la buia   104
                           Passando sopra un ponte   106

IV HERMETIC POETS

GIUSEPPE UNGARETTI   translated by Lowry Nelson, Jr.
                                                         Agonia   110
                                               In memoria   110
                                    Sono una creatura   112
                                                 I fiumi   114
                                                 L'isola   118
                                              La pietà   120
                                         Tu ti spezzasti   126
         Cori descrittivi di stati d'animo di Didone   130
EUGENIO MONTALE   translated by Carlo L. Golino
                                                 Falsetto   132
                                           Dora Markus   134
                                  La casa dei doganieri   138
                                      Sotto la pioggia   140
                                           Eastbourne   142
                                   Notizie dall'Amiata   146
                                               L'arca   148
                                      Giorno e notte   150
                                           L'anguilla   152
LIBERO DE LIBERO   translated by Carlo L. Golino
                                 La mia notte ciociara   154
ALFONSO GATTO   translated by John A. Scott
                                         Erba e latte   158
                                        Morto ai paesi   158
                           Piangerà chi non piange   160

Mario Luzi   translated by Carlo L. Golino
                              Avorio   164
                      Donna in Pisa   164
                       Vino e ocra   166
Vittorio Sereni   translated by Carlo L. Golino
                         3 Dicembre   170
                          Terrazza   170
                     Ma se tu manchi   172

V   SALVATORE QUASIMODO—toward transition
Translations by Allen Mandelbaum
                      Vento a Tindari   176
                      Antico inverno   178
                   Strada di Agrigentum   178
                      Òboe sommerso   180
         Di fresca donna riversa in mezzo ai fiori   182
                      Ed è subito sera   182
                   Imitazione della gioia   184
                  Già la pioggia è con noi   184
         Davanti al simulacro di Ilaria del Carretto   186
                Dalla rocca di Bergamo alta   186
                    Quasi un madrigale   188
                     Lettera alla madre   188

VI   NEW TRENDS
Pier Paolo Pasolini   translated by William F. Weaver
                         L'Appennino   194
Margherita Guidacci   translated by Carlo L. Golino
                    Da « Giorno dei Santi »   208

NOTES ON THE POETS   215

I

TWILIGHT POETS

GUIDO GOZZANO

La differenza

Penso e ripenso: — Che mai pensa l'oca
gracidante alla riva del canale?
Pare felice! Al vespero invernale
protende il collo, giubilando roca.

Salta starnazza si rituffa gioca:
nè certo sogna d'essere mortale
nè certo sogna il prossimo Natale
nè l'armi corruscanti della cuoca.

— O pàpera, mia candida sorella,
tu insegni che la Morte non esiste:
solo si muore da che s'è pensato.

Ma tu non pensi. La tua sorte è bella!
Chè l'esser cucinato non è triste,
triste è il pensare d'esser cucinato.

I Colloqui

I

Venticinqu'anni!... Sono vecchio, sono
vecchio! Passò la giovinezza prima,
il dono mi lasciò dell'abbandono!

Translated by Carlo L. Golino

The Difference

I think and think again:—What thinks the goose
on the canal bank croaking with all her might?
She seems happy! In the winter twilight
stretching her neck out jubilant and raucous.

She jumps, dives, flutters her gay wings loose,
and surely doesn't dream how short her flight
and surely doesn't dream of Christmas night
or of the cook's bright weapons and their use.

O gosling, my sister, most candid mate,
Death does not exist, you teach us all:
only as he thought did man begin to die.

But you don't think. Yours is a happy fate!
Since to be fried is not sad at all,
What's sad is the thought that we must fry.

Conversations

I

Twenty-five years! I am old, indeed
I am old! My prime of youth fled fast
and left me only emptiness and need.

Un libro di passato, ov'io reprima
il mio singhiozzo e il pallido vestigio
riconosca di lei, tra rima e rima.

Venticinqu'anni! Medito il prodigio
biblico... guardo il sole che declina
già lentamente sul mio cielo grigio.

Venticinqu'anni... Ed ecco la trentina
inquietante, torbida d'istinti
moribondi... ecco poi la quarantina

spaventosa, l'età cupa dei vinti,
poi la vecchiezza, l'orrida vecchiezza
dai denti finti e dai capelli tinti.

O non assai goduta giovinezza,
oggi ti vedo quale fosti, vedo
il tuo sorriso, amante che s'apprezza

solo nell'ora triste del congedo!
Venticinq'anni!... Come più m'avanzo
all'altra meta, gioventù, m'avvedo

che fosti bella come un bel romanzo!

II

Ma un bel romanzo che non fu vissuto
da me, ch'io vidi vivere da quello
che mi seguì, dal mio fratello muto.

Io piansi e risi per quel mio fratello
che pianse e rise, e fu come lo spettro
ideale di me, giovine e bello.

A ciascun passo mi rivolsi indietro,
curioso di lui, con occhi fissi
spiando il suo pensiero, or gaio or tetro.

A book of time gone by, wherein my last
sobs may be repressed, where its paling trace
I may recognize in rimes of my past.

Twenty-five years! Within my thoughts I embrace
the biblical wonder . . . on my greying sky
I watch the sun go down with slow pace.

Twenty-five years . . . Then thirty will go by
disquieting, with murky instincts allied
to death . . . till forty will draw nigh

frightful—forty, the gloomy age of tried
and vanquished men; then horrid old age,
old age with its false teeth and its hair dyed.

O never-enough-enjoyed youthful age,
I see today what you really were, well
I see your smile, lover whose charms engage

us only in the sad hour of farewell!
Twenty-five years! . . . the more I advance
to other destinations, O youth, clearly I can tell

yours was the beauty of a fair romance!

II
But a fair romance not lived by me. Another
one whom I have watched has lived it, one
who followed me and was my silent brother.

As he cried and laughed so I have done
for him, my brother, who was the ideal ghost
of me, young, handsome, second to none.

I turned back at every step at most
curiously regarding him with steady eye,
spying his thoughts, now sad, now full of boast.

Egli pensò le cose ch'io ridissi,
confortò la mia pena in sè romita,
e visse quella vita che non vissi.

Egli ama e vive la sua dolce vita;
non io che, solo nei miei sogni d'arte,
narrai la bella favola compita.

Non vissi. Muto sulle mute carte
ritrassi lui, meravigliando spesso.
Non vivo. Solo, gelido, in disparte,

sorrido e guardo vivere me stesso.

L'assenza

Un bacio. Ed è lungi. Dispare
giù in fondo, là dove si perde
la strada boschiva, che pare
un gran corridoio nel verde.

Risalgo qui dove dianzi
vestiva il bell'abito grigio:
rivedo l'uncino, i romanzi
ed ogni sottile vestigio....

Mi piego al balcone. Abbandono
la gota sopra la ringhiera.
E non sono triste. Non sono
più triste. Ritorna stasera.

E intorno declina l'estate.
E sopra un geranio vermiglio,
fremendo le ali caudate
si libra un enorme Papilio....

He thought the things I said. He for my
lonely sorrow was the comfort, he had
the life I never lived as time went by.

He loves and lives his sweet life and led
this life, not I, who only in my dreams of art
have told my fairy-tale in charming words perfected.

I did not live. In silence with a silent heart
I painted him, often with wonder rife.
I don't live. Alone, cold, in the stranger's part,

I smile, watching myself living my life.

Absence

A kiss. She is gone. Disappearing
there, where in the wooded thickness
the path loses itself reappearing
as a long corridor in the greenness.

Again I climb up here, again I look
where she stood now garbed in grey;
I see the novels and the crochet hook,
all the subtle traces of her day . . .

I lean upon the balcony, I lay
languidly my cheek upon the rail.
I am not sad. No longer sad in any way.
Tonight she will be back without fail.

Around me summer is declining.
On a geranium vermilion-bright,
with tailed wings frantically vibrating
a butterfly, immense, soars into flight . . .

L'azzurro infinito del giorno
è come una seta ben tesa;
ma sulla serena distesa
la luna già pensa al ritorno.

Lo stagno risplende. Si tace
la rana. Ma guizza un bagliore
d'acceso smeraldo, di brace
azzurra: il martin pescatore....

E non sono triste. Ma sono
stupito se guardo il giardino....
stupito di che? non mi sono
sentito mai tanto bambino....

Stupito di che? Delle cose.
I fiori mi paiono strani:
ci sono pur sempre le rose,
ci sono pur sempre i gerani....

The infinite blueness of the day
is like a piece of silk stretched tight;
but on the serene vastness of light
the moon already plans another stay.

The pond shines bright. Silent becomes
the frog. But a gleam of burning
emerald, of bluish embers comes
flashing: the kingfisher is running . . .

And I am not sad. But as I am gazing
upon the garden, I am more and more
amazed . . . What is to me amazing?
I've never felt such a child before . . .

Amazed at what? At what exists.
The flowers seem strange to me:
Yet roses will always be,
Yet geraniums will always be . . .

SERGIO CORAZZINI

Desolazione
del povero poeta sentimentale

I

Perché tu mi dici: poeta?
Io non sono un poeta.
Io non sono che un piccolo fanciullo che piange.
Vedi: non ho che le lagrime da offrire al Silenzio.
Perché tu mi dici: poeta?

II

Le mie tristezze sono povere tristezze comuni.
Le mie gioie furono semplici,
semplici, così, che se io dovessi confessarle a te arrossirei.
Oggi io penso a morire.

III

Io voglio morire, solamente, perché sono stanco;
solamente perché i grandi angioli
su le vetrate delle catedrali
mi fanno tremare d'amore e di angoscia;
solamente perché, io sono, oramai,
rassegnato come uno specchio,
come un povero specchio melanconico.

Vedi che io non sono un poeta:
sono un fanciullo triste che ha voglia di morire.

Translated by Ronald Farrar

*Desolation
of the Poor Sentimental Poet*

I

Why do you say to me: poet?
I'm not a poet.
I'm only a very small child, crying.
You see: I've nothing but tears to offer the Silence.
Why do you say to me: poet?

II

Even my sorrows are everyone's poor common sorrows.
My pleasures were such simple ones;
Simple, so simple, that if I were to confess them to you I would blush.
Today I am thinking of dying.

III

I want to die, simply because I am tired;
simply because the towering angels
in the stained glass of the cathedrals
make me tremble with love and with anguish.
Simply because I'm resigned now,
as a looking-glass is,
as a poor sad looking-glass is.

You see that I'm not a poet:
I'm a sad little child who wants to die.

IV

Oh, non maravigliarti della mia tristezza!
E non domandarmi;
io non saprei dirti che parole così vane,
Dio mio, così vane,
che mi verrebbe di piangere come se fossi per morire.
Le mie lagrime avrebbero l'aria
di sgranare un rosaio di tristezza
davanti alla mia anima sette volte dolente
ma io non sarei un poeta;
sarei, semplicemente un dolce e pensoso fanciullo
cui avvenisse di pregare, così, come canta e come dorme.

V

Io mi comunico del silenzio, cotidianamente come di Gesù.
E i sacerdoti del silenzio sono i romori,
poi che senza di essi io non avrei cercato e trovato il **Dio**.

VI

Questa notte ho dormito con le mani in croce.
Mi sembrò di essere un piccolo e dolce fanciullo
dimenticato da tutti gli umani,
povera tenera preda del primo venuto;
e desiderai di essere venduto,
di essere battuto
di essere costretto a digiunare
per potermi mettere a piangere tutto solo,
disperatamente triste,
in un angolo oscuro.

VII

Io amo la vita semplice delle cose.
Quante passioni vidi sfogliarsi, a poco a poco,
per ogni cosa che se ne andava!
Ma tu non mi comprendi e sorridi,
e pensi che io sia malato.

IV

Oh, don't be surprised at my sadness!
And don't ask me about it;
I could only answer you with words so useless,
Oh God, so useless,
that I would begin to weep as though I were about to die.
My tears could slowly squeeze themselves out
in a rosary of sadness
seven times before my sorrowing soul
but I wouldn't be a poet;
I would only be a sweet and thoughtful child
who might happen to pray, just as he sings and as he sleeps.

V

I receive communion with silence, every day, just as I do with Jesus.
And the priests of silence are the sounds,
for without them I'd not have looked for and found God.

VI

Last night I slept with my hands in a cross.
And it seemed to me that I was a sweet little child
forgotten by every human being,
a poor helpless prey for the first to come;
I wanted to be sold,
to be beaten,
to be made to starve,
so that I might weep all alone,
desperately sad,
in a dark corner.

VII

I love the simple life of common things.
How many passions have I seen deflower themselves, little by little,
for every single thing that slipped away!
But you don't understand me and you smile,
and think that I'm ill.

VIII

Oh, io sono veramente malato!
E muoio, un poco, ogni giorno.
Vedi: come le cose.
Non sono, dunque, un poeta:
io so che per esser detto poeta, conviene
viver ben altra vita!
Io non so, Dio mio, che morire.
Amen.

Per organo di Barberia

I

Elemosina triste
di vecchie arie sperdute,
vanità di un'offerta
che nessuno raccoglie!
Primavera di foglie
in una via deserta!
Poveri ritornelli
che passano e ripassano
e sono come uccelli
di un cielo musicale!
Ariette d'ospedale
che ci sembra domandino
un'eco in elemosina!

II

Vedi: nessuno ascolta.
Sfogli la tua tristezza
monotona davanti
alla piccola casa
provinciale che dorme;
singhiozzi quel tuo brindisi

VIII

Oh, I am, truly ill!
And I die, a little bit, every day.
You see? just as all things do.
And so, I'm not a poet:
I know that to be called a poet
I would have to live a very different life!
All I know, dear God, is how to die.
Amen.

For Hurdy-Gurdy

I

Sad alms
of old forgotten airs,
vanity of an offering
which no one accepts!
A springtime of leaves
in a deserted street!
Poor melodies
which pass and pass again
and are like birds
in a musical sky!
Little hospital tunes
that seem to beg us
for an echo as an alm.

II

See: no one is listening.
You shed your monotoned
sadness in front of
the small sleeping house
there in the province;
you sob your salute,

folle di agonizzanti
una seconda volta,
ritorni su' tuoi pianti
ostinati di povero
fanciullo incontentato,
e nessuno ti ascolta.

wild as of dying men,
a second time;
again you cry your tears
obstinate like those
of a poor, unsatisfied child,
and no one listens.

II

FUTURISM AND *LA VOCE*

CORRADO GOVONI

Paesi

Esplodon le simpatiche campane
d'un bianco campanile, sopra tetti
grigi: donne, con rossi fazzoletti,
cavano da un rotondo forno il pane.

Ammazzano un maiale nella neve,
tra un gruppo di bambini affascinati
dal sangue, che, con gli occhi spalancati,
aspettan la crudele agonia breve.

Gettano i galli vittoriosi squilli.
I buoi escono dai fienili neri;
si sporgono su l'argine tranquilli,

scendono a bere, gravi, acqua d'argento.
Nei campi, rosei, bianchi, i cimiteri
sperano in mezzo al verde del frumento.

Bellezze

Il campo di frumento è così bello
solo perchè ci sono dentro
i fiori di papavero e di veccia;
ed il tuo volto pallido,

Translated by Carlo L. Golino

Towns

From friendly bells of a white bell-tower
explosive peals go forth over gray roofs:
red-kerchiefed women are taking bread
out of a round oven.

They are killing a pig out in the snow;
spellbound by the blood, children
watch with wide-open eyes, awaiting
the brief moment of cruel agony.

The roosters sing out in victory.
From black haystacks come oxen
and calmly gaze over the bank,

heavily they descend to drink of the silver water.
In the fields the pink, white cemeteries,
amid the greenness of the wheat, lie hoping.

Beauty

The field of wheat is of such beauty
only because within it are found
flowers of vetch and poppy;
and your pale face has beauty only

perchè è tirato un poco indietro
dal peso della lunga treccia.

La trombettina

Ecco che cosa resta
di tutta la magia della fiera:
quella trombettina,
di latta azzurra e verde,
che suona una bambina
camminando, scalza, per i campi.
Ma, in quella nota sforzata,
ci sono dentro i pagliacci bianchi e rossi,
c'è la banda d'oro rumoroso,
la giostra coi cavalli, l'organo, i lumini.
Come, nel sgocciolare della gronda,
c'è tutto lo spavento della bufera,
la bellezza dei lampi e dell'arcobaleno;
nell'umido cerino d'una lucciola
che si sfa su una foglia di brughiera,
tutta la meraviglia della primavera.

because the weight of long tresses
ever so gently tilts it back.

The Little Trumpet

All that is left
of the magic of the fair
is this little trumpet
of blue and green tin,
blown by a girl
as she walks, barefoot, through the fields.
But within its forced note
are all the clowns, white ones and red ones,
the band all dressed in gaudy gold,
the merry-go-round, the calliope, the lights.
Just as in the dripping of the gutter
is all the fearfulness of the storm
the beauty of lightning and the rainbow;
and in the damp flickers of a firefly
whose light dissolves on a heather branch
is all the wondrousness of spring.

ALDO PALAZZESCHI

La fontana malata

Clof, clop, cloch,
cloffete,
cloppete,
clocchete,
chchch....

È giù nel
cortile
la povera
fontana
malata,
che spasimo
sentirla
tossire!
Tossisce,
tossisce,
un poco
si tace,
di nuovo
tossisce.
Mia povera
fontana,
il male
che ài
il cuore
mi preme.

Translated by Carlo L. Golino

The Ailing Fountain

Clof, clop, clok,
cloffity,
cloppity
clockity,
ckckck . . .

Down in the
courtyard
is the poor
ailing
fountain,
such anguish
to hear it
cough!
It coughs,
and coughs;
for a while
it is silent,
then again
it coughs.
Poor fountain
of mine,
you're ailing
and wringing
my heart.

ALDO PALAZZESCHI

Si tace,
non getta
più nulla,
si tace,
non s'ode
romore
di sorta,
che forse....
sia morta?
Che orrore !
Ah, no !
Rieccola
ancora,
tossisce.

Clof, clop, cloch,
cloffete,
cloppete,
clocchete,
chchch....

La tisi
l'uccide.
Dio santo,
quel suo
eterno
tossire
mi fa
morire,
un poco
va bene,
ma tanto !
Che lagno !
Ma Habel !
Vittoria !
Correte,
chiudete
la fonte,

Silence,
not a drop
from the spout,
silence,
no sound
at all
is heard,
perhaps . . .
it is dead?
Oh, horror!
Ah, no!
There,
again,
it coughs.

Clof, clop, clok,
cloffity,
cloppity,
clockity,
ckckck . . .

Consumption
is killing her.
Heavens,
its eternal
coughing
is death
to me,
a little
is fine,
but so much!
Such whining!
Habel!
Victoria!
Do run,
shut off
the fountain,

mi uccide
quel suo
eterno
tossire !
Andate,
mettete
qualcosa
per farla
finire,
magari....
magari
morire !
Madonna !
Gesù!
Non più,
non più !
Mia povera
fontana
col male
che ài
finisci
vedrai
che uccidi
me pure.

Clof, clop, cloch,
cloffete,
cloppete,
clocchete,
chchch....

Ara Mara Amara

In fondo alla china,
fra gli alti cipressi,
v'è un piccolo prato.

its eternal
coughing
is killing
me!
Go, go,
do something,
to make
it stop,
or even . . .
or even
to make it
die!
O Mary!
O Lord!
No more,
no more!
Poor fountain
of mine,
your illness
you'll see,
will be
also
the death
of me.

Clof, clop, clok,
cloffity,
cloppity,
clockity,
ckckck . . .

Ara Mara Amara

At the foot of the slope
among the tall cypress,
there is a small meadow.

Si stanno in quell'ombra
tre vecchie
giocando coi dadi.
Non alzan la testa un istante,
non cambian di posto un sol giorno.
Sull'erba in ginocchio
si stanno in quell'ombra giocando.

Rio Bo

Tre casettine
dai tetti aguzzi,
un verde praticello,
un esiguo ruscello: Rio Bo,
un vigile cipresso.
Microscopico paese, è vero,
paese da nulla, ma però....
c'è sempre di sopra una stella,
una grande, magnifica stella,
che a un dipresso....
occhieggia con la punta del cipresso
di Rio Bo.
Una stella innammorata !
Chi sa
se nemmeno ce l'à
una grande città.

Novembre

Dei giovani e dei vecchi
si raggruppano
fra le rovine calde di Roma,
su cui i platani lasciano cadere
con rumore di carta

There in that shade
are three old women
playing dice.
They never raise their heads for a moment,
nor do they change their places any day.
On their knees, on the grass,
they stay in that shade, and play.

Rio Bo

Three little houses
with pointed roofs,
a green little meadow,
a smallish brook: Rio Bo,
a vigilant cypress.
Microscopic town, it is true,
insignificant town, but still . . .
up above there is always a star,
a large, magnificent star,
which somehow . . .
flirts with the top of the cypress
of Rio Bo.
A star in love!
Who knows
if even a great city afar
possesses such a star.

November

Some young and old men
gather
among warm Roman ruins
on which the plane trees shed
their golden leaves

le loro foglie dorate.
I giovani fanno sapere ai vecchi
quello che a loro piace,
e i vecchi fanno finta di non sentire.

Il Palatino

Sui morbidi cuscini del tempo
il corpo riposa
nel torrido meriggio d'estate.
Il pensiero non ha la forza di evocare
né ombre né fantasmi,
e l'occhio a pena sorprende
dei vapori trasparenti
che salgono dalla terra
e che il calore discioglie nella luce.
Bevute dal sole
le pietre sono bianche
come tombe anonime e deserte,
e le fronde palpitano leggere
di un'aspirazione celeste.
Pel cocente abbandono
i sensi percepiscono soltanto un profumo.
Il presente puzza
e il futuro è termine vago,
il passato non puzza più,
ha un vago profumo di foglie secche
il passato.

with a sound of paper falling.
The young inform the old
of things they like,
the old men pretend not to hear.

The Palatine

On the soft cushions of time
the body rests
in the torrid summer afternoon.
Thought has no strength to conjure up
phantoms or ghosts,
the eye just glimpses
transparent vapors
rising from the earth
dissolved by heat into the light.
Drunk by the sun
the stones are white
as tombs anonymous and deserted,
the branches quiver lightly
in celestial desire.
Through burning abandon
the senses perceive only a fragrance.
The present is a stench
and the future a vague notion,
the past has lost its stench,
it has a vague fragrance of withered leaves
. . . the past.

GIOVANNI PAPINI

Ottava poesia

Quaderno bianco, principio di giorno,
conto vergine, pagina prima —
non si parli di ritorno
che in cima all'ultima cima.

Chiara di foglie tenere verdezza,
tepido odor di canto per le vie,
ricompensa alla mia grandezza
incoronata di gelosie.

Mai come in questa mattina nuova,
con nuovo cuore martello col passo
la strada, che il corpo ritrova
tra le muraglie doppie di sasso.

Marcio a spinte d'istinto: mi volto
intorno a me, padrone nel deserto;
nel cavo silenzio mi ascolto
parlare convinto ed aperto.

Alla fine, e per sempre, solitario;
lieto, leggero, sigaretta in bocca;
fuor del vero e dell'ordinario
vo dove nulla mi tocca.

Ogni cosa che guardo mi faccio:
son l'ombra del muro, la luce de' lumi

Translated by Carlo L. Golino

Eighth Poem

Blank book, beginning of a day
clean bill, page one—
let no word be spoken of returning
until the summit of the last summit.

Bright greenness of tender leaves,
warm fragrance of songs in the streets,
reward to my greatness
crowned by jealousy.

Never as in this new morning,
with heart renewed I hammer my step
upon the road the body rediscovers,
between the twin walls of stone.

I march at instinct's urge; I look
around me, master of the desert;
in the hollow silence I listen
to my convinced and open words.

Finally, and forever, alone;
happy, lighthearted, cigarette in my mouth,
away from truth and triteness
I go where nothing can touch me.

I become everything I see:
I am the shadow of the wall, the light of lights

il sole respiro ed abbraccio
senza paura che mi consumi.

Son di me stesso l'amato amante,
bacio labbro con labbro, mi stringo
la mano con mano bruciante,
mi posseggo intero e non fingo.

Non siamo più coppia — son l'uno
partorito dal proprio amore;
son chi non cerca nessuno,
sazio appena del suo furore.

Perduto in un sollievo di fantasia,
non c'è, per lo sguardo, orizzonte,
sopra la terra fatta mia,
tutta rinchiusa nella mia fronte.

Carezze d'aria dal cielo al mio viso,
ardente di sommossa volontà,
danno al bandito deriso
l'ultimo tocco di maestà.

Ma quando, al finire del giorno,
ritrovo, stracco e freddo, la fossa della strada,
nella mezzombra lilla del ritorno
sono il povero triste a cui nessuno bada.

I breathe, embrace the sun
not fearful of any harm.

I am the beloved lover of myself,
I kiss lip with lip, I squeeze
one hand with a burning hand,
fully I possess myself, I don't pretend.

We are no longer a couple—I am the one
born of his own love;
I am the one who needs no other
barely sated by his own furor.

Lost in fancy's consolations
for my eye there is no horizon
upon the earth, my own,
wholly enclosed within my brow.

Heaven's airy caresses upon my face,
burning with a riotous will,
add to the derided outcast
a last touch of majesty.

But when at day's end,
tired and cold, I find again the road's ditch,
in the lilac dusk of my return
I am the sad creature nobody heeds.

CLEMENTE RÈBORA

Campana di Lombardia

Campana di Lombardia,
Voce tua, voce mia,
Voce voce che vai via
E non dài malinconia.
Io non so che cosa sia,
Se tacendo o risonando
Vien fiducia verso l'alto
Di guarir l'intimo pianto,
Se nel petto è melodia
Che domanda e che risponde,
Se in pannocchie di armonia
Risplendendo si trasfonde
Cuore a cuore, voce a voce —
Voce, voce che vai via
E non dài malinconia.

Dall'immagine tesa

Dall'immagine tesa
Vigilo l'istante
Con imminenza d'attesa —
E non aspetto nessuno:
Nell'ombra accesa
Spio il campanello

Translated by Carlo L. Golino

Lombardy Bell

Lombardy bell,
Voice of mine and yours as well,
Voice that fading casts a spell
Quick all sadness to dispel.
Why it is I cannot tell,
If you're still or if you're heard
Faith in Heaven with new bonds
Bids us close our inner wounds,
If a melody in our breast
Posing queries then replying,
Into harmony were cast
Its resplendent change complying
Heart to heart, voice to voice—
Voice that fading casts a spell
Quick all sadness to dispel.

With Tense Imagination

With tense imagination
I count the seconds
In imminent expectation—
But I await no one:
In the lighted shadows
I watch the bell

Che impercettibile spande
Un polline di suono —
E non aspetto nessuno:
Fra quattro mura
Stupefatte di spazio
Più che un deserto
Non aspetto nessuno.
Ma deve venire,
Verrà, se resisto
A sbocciare non visto,
Verrà d'improvviso,
Quando meno l'avverto,
Verrà quasi perdono
Di quanto fa morire,
Verrà a farmi certo,
Del suo e mio tesoro,
Verrà come ristoro
Delle mie e sue pene,
Verrà, forse già viene
Il suo bisbiglio.

As it imperceptibly grows
Into fluttering sounds—
But I await no one:
Within four walls
Overwhelming with space
More than a desert
I await no one.
But come it must,
It will, if holding fast,
Unseen, till my hour I last.
Suddenly it will come
When least expected.
It will come as forgiveness
For all it yields to death,
It will come as reassurance
Of mine, of its rewards,
It will come as sweet relief
To sorrows we both share,
It will come, perhaps its whisper
Has come already.

PIERO JAHIER

Serata

Mi sono bardato per la serata
(dal momento che volete vedermi
nei vestiti che gridano: non è lui)
Io che respiravo alle giunture degli abiti vecchi
come un insetto
Mi son bardato per la serata.

E — tremando — dall'anticamera riscaldata
mi son prodotto nella luce, negli specchi e sorrisi
— un sorcio traversa il salone
del transatlantico —

E nuotando nella luce, negli specchi e sorrisi
dell'accoglienza cordiale
mi son trovato a parlare
delle sole cose care
a spiegare e difender la causa della mia vita.

Ma ho visto — a tempo —
il respiro della mia passione
congelarsi contro i vostri visi
A tempo mi avete guardato
come un drago che butta fuoco.

Mi domando perché mi avete invitato.

Translated by Carlo L. Golino

Evening Party

I have put on my trappings for the evening
(since you want to see me
in clothes that cry out: it is not he)
I, who breathed through the seams of worn clothes
like an insect
I have put on my trappings for the evening.

And—trembling—from the heated anteroom
I showed myself into the light, into the mirrors, into the smiles
—a mouse crosses the ballroom
of the steamship—

And floating in the light, in the mirrors, in the smiles
of a cordial reception
I found myself speaking
of the only things I cherish
explaining and defending the cause of my life.

But I saw—just in time—
the breath of my feelings
freezing against your faces
Just in time you looked at me
as if I were a fire-spitting dragon.

I ask myself why you invited me.

Ma se è perché ho scritto
tre parole sincere
e vorreste il segreto
di questo mestiere:
ci son sette porte
e ho perso la chiave
per poterci tornare
Se le ho dette, vuol dire che avran traboccato
Alzatevi presto
e vedrete alzarsi la lodola
quando il sole ha chiamato.

Nella via mentre rincasate
su molle compensate
ritrovo la mia chiave, solo.

Sono stato visitato
sono stato auscultato
riconosciuto abile a vita coraggiosa.

Dieci volte respinto
ricomincerò
E se proprio fossi disteso
una polla di sangue al petto
aspettate a venirmi vicino
ancora non vi accostate....

Ma ho ritrovato la mia chiave
solo
ma vi ringrazio
ma son tornato dove non potete venire
dove son certo che la mia parola
senza averla gridata
non posso
morire.

If it is because I have written
a few sincere words
and you want the secret
of this, my trade:
there are seven doors
and I have lost the key
to enter again
If I said them, it means they simply overflowed
Get up early
and you will see the lark
when the sun has beckoned.

On the way home as you ride
on cushioned springs
I again find my key, alone.

I have been examined
I have been observed
and found fit for a fearless life.

Ten times rejected
I will begin again
And if I were to be stretched out
a pool of blood upon my chest
wait to draw near me
do not as yet approach . . .

For I have found the key again
alone
and I thank you
for I have returned where you cannot come
where I am certain that if
I do not speak my word
I cannot
die.

PIERO JAHIER

CAMILLO SBARBARO

Taci, anima stanca di godere

Taci, anima stanca di godere
e di soffrire (all'uno e all'altro vai
rassegnata).
Ascolto e non mi giunge una tua voce
non di rimpianto per la miserabile
giovinezza, non d'ira e di speranza,
e neppure di tedio.
                      Giaci come
il corpo, ammutolita,
in un'indifferenza disperata.
                    Noi non ci stupiremo
non è vero, mia anima, se il cuore
s'arrestasse, sospeso se ci fosse
il fiato...
                    Invece camminiamo.
Camminiamo io e te come sonnambuli.
E gli alberi, son alberi, le case
son case, le donne
che passano son donne, e tutto è quello
che è, soltanto quel che è.

La vicenda di gioia e di dolore
non ci tocca. Perduta ha la sua voce
la sirena del mondo, e il mondo è un grande
deserto.
                    Nel deserto
io guardo con asciutti occhi me stesso.

Translated by Carlo L. Golino

Be Still My Soul, Weary of Pleasure

Be still my soul, weary of pleasure
and of sorrow (resigned you pass from one
to the other).
I listen but I hear not your voice
not of regret for a wretched
youth, not of wrath or hope,
not even of boredom.   You lie
as the body lies, silent,
in desperate indifference.
        We shall not be astonished,
not so, my soul, if our heart
were to stop, if our breath were
withheld . . .
        Instead we go forward.
We go forward you and I as sleepwalkers.
And the trees, they are trees, the houses
houses, the women
that go by are women, and all is
what it is, only what it is.

Alternating joys and sorrows
do not touch us. The siren of the world
has lost its voice, and the world is a vast
desert.
        In the desert
with dry eyes I behold myself.

DINO CAMPANA

Giardino autunnale

    Al giardino spettrale al lauro muto
De le verdi ghirlande
A la terra autunnale
Un ultimo saluto!
A l'aride pendici
Aspre arrossate nell'estremo sole
Confusa di rumori
Rauchi grida la lontana vita:
Grida al morente sole
Che insanguina le aiole.
S'intende una fanfara
Che straziante sale: il fiume spare
Ne le arene dorate; nel silenzio
Stanno le bianche statue a capo i ponti
Volte: e le cose già non sono piú.
E dal fondo silenzio come un coro
Tenero e grandioso
Sorge ed anela in alto al mio balcone:
E in aroma d'alloro,
In aroma d'alloro acre languente,
Tra le statue immortali nel tramonto
Ella m'appar, presente.

Translated by Carlo L. Golino

Autumn Garden

To the ghostly garden, to the silent laurel
Of the green garlands
To the autumn earth
A last farewell!
To the rugged, barren slopes
Reddening in the setting sun,
Distant life cries out
In confusion of harsh sounds:
It cries to the dying sun
That stains the flower beds blood-red.
A flourish of trumpets is heard
Rising piercingly; the river disappears
In the golden sand; silently, their heads turned,
The white statues stand at the end of the bridges:
And things are no more.
Something like a tender, majestic chorus
Of the deep silence
Reaches high, panting, up to my balcony:
And amidst the fragrance of the laurel,
The laurel's lingering, pungent scent,
Among the immortal statues in the sunset
She appears to me, present.

La chimera

Non so se tra roccie il tuo pallido
Viso m'apparve, o sorriso
Di lontananze ignote
Fosti, la china eburnea
Fronte fulgente o giovine
Suora de la Gioconda:
O delle primavere
Spente, per i tuoi mitici pallori
O Regina o Regina adolescente:
Ma per il tuo ignoto poema
Di voluttà e di dolore
Musica fanciulla esangue,
Segnato di linea di sangue
Nel cerchio delle labbra sinuose,
Regina de la melodia:
Ma per il vergine capo
Reclino, io poeta notturno
Vegliai le stelle vivide nei pelaghi del cielo,
Io per il tuo dolce mistero
Io per il tuo divenir taciturno.
Non so se la fiamma pallida
Fu dei capelli il vivente
Segno del suo pallore,
Non so se fu un dolce vapore,
Dolce sul mio dolore,
Sorriso di un volto notturno:
Guardo le bianche rocce le mute fonti dei venti
E l'immobilità dei firmamenti
E i gonfi rivi che vanno piangenti
E l'ombre del lavoro umano curve là sui poggi algenti
E ancora per teneri cieli lontane chiare ombre correnti
E ancora ti chiamo ti chiamo Chimera.

The Chimera

I know not if among rocks
Your pale face appeared to me
Or if the smile
Of distances unknown you were,
Your radiant ivory brow inclined,
O young Sister of the Gioconda:
Or of spent springtimes,
And by your mythic pallor,
O Queen, adolescent Queen:
But for your unknown poem
Of voluptuousness and grief,
Marked by a line of blood
In the circle of sinuous lips,
Musical deathly-pale girl,
Queen of melody:
But for the virginal head
Downbent, I poet of the night
Kept vigil at the bright stars in the depths of heaven,
I for your sweet mystery
I for your silent unfolding.
I know not
If the pale flame of her hair
Was the living sign of her pallor,
I know not if it was a sweet vapor
Sweet to my sorrow,
A smile upon a face out of the night.
I gaze upon white rocks the winds' silent sources
Upon the immobility of firmaments
Upon the swollen rivers that flow weeping
Upon the shadows of human labor kneeling over the icy hills
Upon distant clear shades fleeting through tender skies
And still I call to you I call to you Chimera.

Viaggio a Montevideo

Io vidi dal ponte della nave
I colli di Spagna
Svanire, nel verde
Dentro il crepuscolo d'oro la bruna terra celando
Come una melodia:
D'ignota scena fanciulla sola
Come una melodia
Blu, sulla riva dei colli ancora tremare una viola...
Illanguidiva la sera celeste sul mare:
Pure i dorati silenzii ad ora ad ora dell'ale
Varcaron lentamente in un azzurreggiare:...
Lontani tinti dei varii colori
Dai piú lontani silenzii
Ne la celeste sera varcaron gli uccelli d'oro: la nave
Già cieca varcando battendo la tenebra
Coi nostri naufraghi cuori
Battendo la tenebra l'ale celeste sul mare.
Ma un giorno
Salirono sopra la nave le gravi matrone di Spagna
Da gli occhi torbidi e angelici
Dai seni gravidi di vertigine. Quando
In una baia profonda di un'isola equatoriale
In una baia tranquilla e profonda assai piú del cielo notturno
Noi vedemmo sorgere nella luce incantata
Una bianca città addormentata
Ai piedi dei picchi altissimi dei vulcani spenti
Nel soffio torbido dell'equatore: finché
Dopo molte grida e molte ombre di un paese ignoto,
Dopo molto cigolío di catene e molto acceso fervore
Noi lasciammo la città equatoriale
Verso l'inquieto mare notturno.
Andavamo andavamo, per giorni e per giorni: le navi
Gravi di vele molli di caldi soffi incontro passavano lente:
Sì presso di sul cassero a noi ne appariva bronzina
Una fanciulla della razza nuova,

Voyage to Montevideo

From the ship's deck I saw
The hills of Spain
Vanish, into the golden dusk
Concealing the brown earth with greenness
Like a melody:
On the bank of the hills I saw a violet still quivering,
Solitary creature of an unknown view
Like a blue melody . . .
Over the sea the azure evening lingered:
Still now and then a flutter of wings
Crossed slowly the golden silence fading into the blue: . . .
In the distance, tinted in many hues
The golden birds flew across the blue evening
Out of the remotest silence; the ship
Already sailing blindly, battering the darkness
Its blue wing upon the sea, battering the darkness
With our shipwrecked hearts.
Then one day
The solemn Spanish matrons came aboard
With eyes turbid, angelic,
Their breasts heavy with vertigo. Then
In a peaceful bay far deeper than the sky of night
We saw rising through the enchanted light
A slumbering white city
Below the highest peaks of spent volcanoes
In the equator's turbid breath: until
After much shouting and many shadows of a land unknown
After much rattling of chains and much heated toil
We left the equatorial city
For the restless sea at night.
We sailed and sailed, day after day: ships
Heavy with sail limp in the warm breezes passed slowly by:
Nearby on the quarter-deck appeared to us, bronzed
A girl of the new race,

Occhi lucenti e le vesti al vento! ed ecco: selvaggia a la fine di un
                                           giorno che apparve
La riva selvaggia là giú sopra la sconfinata marina:
E vidi come cavalle
Vertiginose che si scioglievano le dune
Verso la prateria senza fine
Deserta senza le case umane
E noi volgemmo fuggendo le dune che apparve
Su un mare giallo de la portentosa dovizia del fiume,
Del continente nuovo la capitale marina.
Limpido fresco ed elettrico era il lume
Della sera e là le alte case parevan deserte
Laggiú sul mar del pirata
De la città abbandonata
Tra il mare giallo e le dune...
. . . .

Donna genovese

Tu mi portasti un po' d'alga marina
Nei tuoi capelli, ed un odor di vento,
Che è corso di lontano e giunge grave
D'ardore, era nel tuo corpo bronzino:
— Oh la divina
Semplicità delle tue forme snelle —
Non amore non spasimo, un fantasma,
Un'ombra della necessità che vaga
Serena e ineluttabile per l'anima
E la discioglie in gioia, in incanto serena
Perché per l'infinito lo scirocco
Se la possa portare.
Come è piccolo il mondo e leggero nelle tue mani!

Her eyes shining, her clothes to the wind! and then: wild at the end
of the day appeared
The wild shore there upon the endless beach:
And I saw the dunes
Like speeding mares dissolving
Into the endless prairie
Devoid of human abode.
And we turned fleeing the dunes, and there appeared
Upon the yellow sea of the river's prodigious wealth
The marine capital of the new continent.
Limpid, cool and artificial was the light
Of evening and there the tall houses seemed deserted
Down on the pirates' sea
Of the abandoned city
Between the yellow sea and the dunes . . .
. . . .

Woman from Genoa

You brought me a cluster of seaweed
In your hair, and a fragrance of wind
That travels from afar laden with passion
Was in your body bronzed by the sun:
—Oh the divine
Simplicity of your slender body—
Not love not anguish, but a phantom,
A shadow of compulsion that wanders
Inevitable and serene into the soul,
Dissolving it into joy, into serene enchantment,
So that the sirocco
May carry it away in endless space.
How small the world is, how light in your hands!

Due liriche per S. A.

Vi amai nella città dove per sole
Strade si posa il passo illanguidito
Dove una pace tenera che piove
A sera il cuor non sazio e non pentito
Volge a un'ambigua primavera in viole
Lontane sopra il cielo impallidito.

* * *

In un momento
Sono sfiorite le rose
I petali caduti
Perché io non potevo dimenticare le rose
Le cercavamo insieme
Abbiamo trovato delle rose
Erano le sue rose erano le mie rose
Questo viaggio chiamavamo amore
Col nostro sangue e colle nostre lacrime facevamo le rose
Che brillavano un momento al sole del mattino
Le abbiamo sfiorite sotto il sole tra i rovi
Le rose che non erano le nostre rose
Le mie rose le sue rose.

P.S. — E cosí dimenticammo le rose.

L'invetriata

La sera fumosa d'estate
Dall'alta invetriata mesce chiarori nell'ombra
E mi lascia nel cuore un suggello ardente.
Ma chi ha (sul terrazzo sul fiume si accende una lampada) chi ha
A la Madonnina del Ponte chi è chi è che ha acceso la lampada? — c'è
Nella stanza un odor di putredine: c'è
Nella stanza una piaga rossa languente.

Two Lyrics for S. A.

I loved you in the lone streets of the city
Where the steps fall with a languid rhythm
Where tender peace, like rain upon the evening,
Turns the insatiate unrepentant heart
To a vague springtime of violets remote
Above the sky suddenly grown pale.

* * *

In one moment
The roses have faded
The petals fallen
Because I could not forget the roses
We searched for them together
We found roses
That were her roses, my roses
This journey we called love
Out of our blood and tears we made roses
That shone but a moment in the morning sun
Under the sun among the briars we withered the roses
That were not our roses
Roses that were not mine, not hers.

P.S.: And thus we forgot the roses.

The Skylight

From the skylight up high
The smoky summer evening pours brightness into shadows
Leaving upon my heart a burning seal.
But who (a lamp is lit on the terrace over the river), who has,
For our gentle Lady of the Bridge, who, who has lit the lamp?—
                                                    there is
In the room an odor of decay; there is
In the room a red lingering wound.

Le stelle sono bottoni di madreperla e la sera si veste di velluto:
E tremola la sera fatua: è fatua la sera e tremola ma c'è
Nel cuore della sera c'è,
Sempre una piaga rossa languente.

The stars are buttons of mother-of-pearl, the evening is cloaked
in velvet:
The fatuous evening is trembling; the evening is fatuous and
trembling but there is
In the heart of the evening there is
Always a red lingering wound.

III

TRADITION AND EXPERIMENT

UMBERTO SABA

La capra

Ho parlato a una capra.
Era sola sul prato, era lagata.
Sazia d'erbe, bagnata
dalla pioggia, belava.

Quell'uguale belato era fraterno
al mio dolore. Ed io risposi, prima
per celia, poi perchè il dolore è eterno,
ha una voce e non varia.
Questa voce sentivo
gemere in una capra solitaria.

In una capra dal viso semita
sentivo querelarsi ogni altro male,
ogni altra vita.

« Frutta erbaggi »

Erbe, frutta colori della bella
stagione. Poche ceste ove alla sete
si rivelano dolci polpe crude.

Entra un fanciullo colle gambe nude,
imperioso, fugge via.

Translated by Thomas G. Bergin

The Goat

I have spoken with a goat.
She was alone in the meadow, tied to a post.
Satiated with grass and her coat
rain-sodden, she was bleating.

The incessant bleat I felt blending
with my own grief and I answered,
in mockery first and then after
(for sorrow timeless unending
has but the one unvarying note)
because of the message that came
borne over the field from the goat.

From a goat with semitic muzzle
I heard the lamenting
of all living things and their trouble.

"Fruit and Greens"

Green goods, fruit, the colors of the fairest
season. Some wicker baskets that display
the sweet raw fibers, tempting to the tooth.

Enter, brown legs flashing bare, a youth,
imperious, then darts away.

　　　　　　S'oscura
l'umile botteguccia, invecchia come
una madre.
　　　　　　　Di fuori egli nel sole
si allontana, con l'ombra sua, leggero.

Ulisse

Nella mia giovanezza ho navigato
lungo le coste dalmate. Isolotti
a fior d'onda emergevano, ove raro
un uccello sostava intento a prede,
coperti d'alghe, scivolosi, al sole
belli come smeraldi. Quando l'alta
marea e la notte li annullava, vele
sottovento sbandavano più al largo,
per fuggirne l'insidia. Oggi il mio regno
è quella terra di nessuno. Il porto
accende ad altri i suoi lumi; me al largo
sospinge ancora il non domato spirito,
e della vita il doloroso amore.

Donna

Quand'eri
giovinetta pungevi
come una mora di macchia. Anche il piede
t'era un'arma, o selvaggia.

Eri difficile a prendere.

　　　　　　　　Ancora
giovane, ancora

       And darkness
falls on the humble little shop, swift aging
like a mother.
      He, outside, in the sunblaze
slips off, his shadow following, light-footed.

Ulysses

From days of youth I remember sailing
past the Dalmatian shore; the rugged islets
came forth from the waves. On them, but rarely,
sea birds, intent on prey, would alight; the beaches,
kelp-encrusted, gave slippery footing. Under
the sun they sparkled, bright as emeralds.
The tide rising or the dark blotting them out,
barks bearing leeward gave them wide berth,
fleeing their treachery. And now my kingdom
is that land of No-man. The harbor kindles
its light for others. I turn out to sea,
once more impelled by heart untamed and love,
laden with sorrow, of the life of man.

Woman

When you were a girl
you could sting
like the thorn of a wild blackberry.
Your foot, too, little savage,
you wielded as a weapon.

You were hard to take.

      Now still young
you are still lovely, the threads

sei bella. I segni
degli anni, quelli del dolore, legano
l'anime nostre, una ne fanno. E dietro
i capelli nerissimi che avvolgo
alle mie dita, più non temo il piccolo,
bianco puntuto orecchio demoniaco.

Il vetro rotto

Tutto si muove contro te. Il maltempo,
le luci che si spengono, la vecchia
casa scossa a una raffica e a te cara
per il male sofferto, le speranze
deluse, qualche bene in lei goduto.
Ti pare il sopravvivere un rifiuto
d'obbedienza alle cose.
     E nello schianto
del vetro alla finestra è la condanna.

L'arboscello

Oggi il tempo è di pioggia.
Sembra il giorno una sera,
sembra la primavera
un autunno, ed un gran vento devasta
l'arboscello che sta — e non pare — saldo;
par tra le piante un giovanetto alto
troppo per la sua troppo verde età.
Tu lo guardi. Hai pietà
forse di tutti quei candidi fiori
che la bora gli toglie; e son frutta,
son dolci conserve
per l'inverno quei fiori che tra l'erbe

of years and sorrow bind together
our souls, and make them one. No longer
under the jet-black strands that my fingers
gather in do I fear
the little white faunlike keen-pointed ear.

The Broken Glass

All things take arms against you. The bad weather,
the lights that go out of themselves, and, shuddering
under the bluster of the storm, the old house,
dear for the ills it sheltered and the hopes
deluded, the few happy hours as well.
You feel survival would mean to rebel
against the law of things.
                                      And in the crash
of splintering pane your sentence is pronounced.

The Young Tree

Today the weather brings us rain;
Evening it seems, not day,
our springtime, you would say,
in autumn, and a wind arises, wasting
the little tree which seems to yield, yet stands
firm, like a slender youth, among the plants,
too tall for his green immaturity.
You look out, and maybe
feel pity for the candid blossoms stripped
and borne off by the gale. The summer's fruit,
the winter's sugared jams
die with those flowers scattered on the grass;

cadono. E se ne duole la tua vasta
maternità.

Felicità

La giovanezza cupida di pesi
porge spontanea al carico le spalle.
Non regge. Piange di malinconia.

Vagabondaggio, evasione, poesia,
cari prodigi sul tardi! Sul tardi
l'aria si affina ed i passi si fanno
leggeri.
Oggi è il meglio di ieri,
se non è ancora la felicità.

Assumeremo un giorno la bontà
del suo volto, vedremo alcuno sciogliere
come un fumo il suo inutile dolore.

Ceneri

Ceneri
di cose morte, di mali perduti,
di contatti ineffabili, di muti
sospiri;

vivide
fiamme da voi m'investono nell'atto
che d'ansia in ansia approssimo alle soglie
del sonno;

e al sonno,
con quei legami appassionati e teneri

and so grief comes to move your all-embracing
maternity.

Happiness

Youth, greedy for burdens,
proffers its willing shoulders for the load.
And cannot bear it. And weeps despairingly.

Wide wanderings, escape, free fantasy:
dear wonders at day's end. At day's end
the air is cleaner, steps move lightly
on the way.
Today is the best of yesterday
even though still it be not happiness.

We shall assume one day the gentleness
of its fair face, and some we shall see cleaving,
as through smoke, their vain grieving.

Ashes

Ashes
of dead things, ills forgotten,
contacts unspeakable, dumb
regrets;

red-glowing
the flames from you envelop me, even as,
borne on from care to care, I near the sill
of sleep.

And so to sleep,
in bonds like those impassioned and yet tender

ch'ànno il bimbo e la madre, ed a voi ceneri
mi fondo.

L'angoscia
insidia del varco, io la disarmo. Come
un beato la via del paradiso,
salgo una scala, sosto ad una porta
a cui suonavo in altri tempi. Il tempo
ha ceduto di colpo.
      Mi sento,
con i panni e con l'anima di allora,
in una luce di folgore; al cuore
una gioia si abbatte vorticosa
come la fine.
    Ma non grido.
         Muto
parto dell'ombre per l'immenso impero.

that bind the child and mother, and to you, **embers**,
I yield.

The anguish
in ambush at the pass I conquer. Like
a blessed soul mounting to Paradise
I climb a stair and pause beside a gate
where once I knocked in other times. The years
have crumbled away.
                      And I feel,
with soul and garments as in bygone days,
a splendor as of lightning; on my heart
in whirling transport exultation breaks . . .
The end then?
                  But I make no outcry.
                                    Mute
I leave the shadows for the vast empire.

VINCENZO CARDARELLI

Estiva

Distesa estate,
stagione dei densi climi
dei grandi mattini
dell'albe senza rumore —
ci si risveglia come in un acquario —
dei giorni identici, astrali,
stagione la meno dolente
d'oscuramenti e di crisi,
felicità degli spazi,
nessuna promessa terrena
può dare pace al mio cuore
quanto la certezza di sole
che dal tuo cielo trabocca,
stagione estrema, che cadi
prostrata in riposi enormi,
dai oro ai piú vasti sogni,
stagione che porti la luce
a distendere il tempo
di là dai confini del giorno,
e sembri mettere a volte
nell'ordine che procede
qualche cadenza dell'indugio eterno.

Translated by Cosimo Corsano

Summertime

Sprawling summer,
season of dense climates,
of broad mornings,
of noiseless dawns—
we awaken to you as in an aquarium—
of identical astral days,
season least grief-stricken
by overcast and tension,
felicity of space,
no one earthly promise
can give peace to my heart
such as the sureness of sunlight
splashing down from your skies,
extreme season that falls
prostrate in huge calms,
you give gold to the vastest dreams,
season that bears the light
to stretch out time
beyond the limits of day
and seems at certain moments to place,
within the order that issues forth,
some cadenza of eternal lingering.

Autunno

Autunno. Già lo sentimmo venire
nel vento d'agosto,
nelle piogge di settembre
torrenziali e piangenti,
e un brivido percorse la terra
che ora, nuda e triste
accoglie un sole smarrito.
Ora passa e declina,
in quest'autunno che incede
con lentezza indicibile,
il miglior tempo della nostra vita
e lungamente ci dice addio.

Adolescente

Su te, vergine adolescente,
sta come un'ombra sacra.
Nulla è piú misterioso
e adorabile e proprio
della tua carne spogliata.
Ma ti recludi nell'attenta veste
e abiti lontano
con la tua grazia,
dove non sai chi ti raggiungerà.
Certo non io. Se ti veggo passare,
a tanta regale distanza
con la chioma sciolta
e tutta la persona astata,
la vertigine mi si porta via.
Sei l'imporosa e liscia creatura
cui preme, nel suo respiro,
l'oscuro gaudio della carne che appena
sopporta la sua pienezza.

Autumn

Autumn. We already felt it coming
in the August wind,
in the September rains,
torrential and weeping,
and a shiver ran through the earth,
that now, bare and sad,
welcomes a bewildered sun.
Now away and down it goes,
in this autumn that is striding
with inexpressibly slow gait,
the best time of our lives,
and it slowly bids us goodbye.

Adolescent

Upon you, adolescent virgin,
a sacred shadow seems to rest.
Nothing is more mysterious
and adorable and unique
than your flesh disrobed.
But you seclude yourself in careful dress,
and with your gracefulness
live in some distant land,
unaware of who will reach you there.
Surely not I. If I behold you walking by,
at such a queenly distance,
with your locks unbound
and your body straight,
vertigo sweeps me away.
You are the impenetrably smooth creature
in whose breathing stirs
the dark bliss of flesh that scarcely
can withstand its plenitude.

Nel sangue, che ha diffusioni
di fiamma, sulla tua faccia,
il cosmo fa le sue risa
come nell'occhio nero della rondine.
La tua pupilla è bruciata
del sole che dentro vi sta.
La tua bocca è serrata.
Non sanno le mani tue bianche
il sudore umiliante dei contatti.
E penso come il tuo corpo,
difficoltoso e vago,
fa disperare l'amore
nel cuor dell'uomo!

Pure qualcuno ti disfiorerà,
bocca di sorgiva.
Qualcuno che non lo saprà,
un pescatore di spugne,
avrà questa perla rara.
Gli sarà grazia e fortuna
il non averti cercata,
e non sapere chi sei
e non poterti godere
con la sottile coscienza
che offende il geloso Iddio.
Oh sí, l'animale sarà
abbastanza ignaro
per non morire prima di toccarti.
E tutto è cosí.
Tu anche non sai chi sei.
E prendere ti lascerai
ma per veder come il gioco è fatto,
per ridere un poco insieme.
Come fiamma si perde nella luce
al tocco della realtà
i misteri che tu prometti
si disciolgono in nulla.

In the blood which fans out wide
in flames upon your face,
the cosmos has its laughter
as in the black eye of a swallow.
Your pupil is seared
by the sun within it.
Your mouth is locked tight.
Those white hands of yours do not know
the shameful sweat of handled flesh.
And I think of how your body,
tortuous and eager,
causes love to despair
in the heart of man!

Yet someone shall deflower you,
O fountainhead.
Someone who will not know it,
a fisherman of sponges,
shall have this priceless pearl.
It shall be a grace and a boon
for him not to have sought you,
and not to know who you are
and not to be able to relish you
with the subtle awareness
that offends a jealous God.
Oh, yes, the animal shall be
sufficiently unaware
not to die before touching you.
And everything is so.
You too know not who you are.
And you shall let yourself be taken
but just to see how the game is played,
just to laugh together a while.
As flame loses itself in the light
at the touch of reality,
the mysteries that you promise
unravel into nothingness.

Inconsumata passerà
tanta gioia!
Tu ti darai, tu ti perderai,
per il capriccio che non indovina
mai, col primo che ti piacerà.
Ama il tempo lo scherzo
che lo seconda,
non il cauto volere che indugia.
Cosí la fanciullezza
fa ruzzolare il mondo,
e il saggio non è che un fanciullo
che si duole di essere cresciuto.

Sera di Gavinana

Ecco la sera e spiove
sul toscano Appennino.
Con lo scender che fan le nubi a valle
prese a lembi qua e là
come ragne fra gli alberi intricate,
si colorano i monti di viola.
Dolce vagare allora
per chi s'affanna il giorno
ed in se stesso, incredulo, si torce.
Viene dai borghi, qui sotto, in faccende,
un vociar lieto e folto in cui si sente
il giorno che declina
e il riposo imminente.
Vi si mischia il pulsare, il batter secco
ed alto del camion sullo stradone
bianco che varca i monti.
E tutto quanto a sera,
grilli, campane, fonti,
fa concerto e preghiera,
trema nell'aria sgombra.

Unconsummated, so much joy
shall fade away!
You shall give yourself, lose yourself,
in a blind caprice that will never
know, with the first to please you.
Time loves the sport of playfulness
that upholds it,
not the cautious wish that dallies.
In such manner does youth
make the world tumble down,
and the sage is nothing but a boy
who grieves because he has grown.

Evening of Gavinana

Here comes the evening and the rains cease
over the Tuscan Apennine.
With the descent of clouds upon the valley,
caught in wisps here and there
like cobwebs in trees, enmeshed,
the hills paint themselves violet.
Sweet wandering at this hour
for those panged by day,
and taut from unbelief within.
From the villages, astir below,
comes a cheerful rumor, humming
with the declining day
and the repose to come.
There mingles the throb and the sharp,
high-pitched beat of the truck on the white
highway that spans the mountains.
And in the evening, all things,
crickets, church bells, fountains
are in concert and in prayer,
trembling in the unencumbered air.

Ma su ogni cosa come piú rifulge,
nell'ora che non ha un'altra luce
il manto dei tuoi fianchi ampi, Appennino.
Sui tuoi prati che salgono a gironi,
questo liquido verde, che rispunta
fra gl'inganni del sole ad ogni acquata,
al vento trascolora e mi rapisce,
per l'inquieto cammino,
sí che teneramente fa star muta
l'anima vagabonda.

Liguria

È la Liguria una terra leggiadra.
Il sasso ardente, l'argilla pulita,
s'avvivano di pampini al sole.
È gigante l'ulivo. A primavera
appar dovunque la mimosa effimera.
Ombra e sole s'alternano
per quelle fonde valli
che si celano al mare,
per le vie lastricate
che vanno in su, fra campi di rose,
pozzi e terre spaccate,
costeggiando poderi e vigne chiuse.
In quell'arida terra il sole striscia
sulle pietre come un serpe.
Il mare in certi giorni
è un giardino fiorito.
Reca messaggi il vento.
Venere torna a nascere
ai soffi del maestrale.
O chiese di Liguria, come navi
disposte a esser varate!
O aperti ai venti e all'onde
liguri cimiteri!

But oh how much the cloak of your broad flanks
outshines all else
this lightless hour, O Apennine!
Upon your meadows rising in spirals,
this limpid green flares up again
betweentimes, when the sun is not beguiled by showers,
changes hue in the winds and wafts me
along the troubled road,
so that with tenderness it hushes
my wayfaring soul.

Liguria

Liguria is a lighthearted land.
The burning rock and the polished clay
quicken with vine tendrils in the sun.
The olive tree is a giant. At springtime,
everywhere, the ephemeral mimosa appears.
Shade and sun move in suite
along those hollow valleys
that hide from the sea,
along the paved roads
that rise up high through fields of roses,
wells, and parceled land,
skirting farms and walled vineyards.
In that arid land the sun crawls
like a snake upon the stones.
On certain days, the sea
is a garden in full bloom.
Messages are borne in the wind.
Once again Venus is born
in gusts of the mistral.
O churches of Liguria, like ships
ready to be launched!
Open to the winds and waves,
Ligurian graveyards!

Una rosea tristezza vi colora
quando di sera, simile ad un fiore
che marcisce, la grande luce
si va sfacendo e muore.

A rose sadness comes to color you,
when in the evening, like a flower
that wilts away, the great light
grows dim and dies.

LUIGI BARTOLINI

Rima del confino

Corso avevo, pel fiume intiera notte
sospirando che l'alba a ogni ora fosse
e nessuno venisse insieme a me
(soltanto il mio silenzio e le mie lacrime);
o pregavo che spentasi ogni ira
l'ombra di me per notte si perdesse
e cercassero altrove e sangue e vittima
sgherri che, invece, cercavano me.

Colori

Nero: sei il Nero Inferno, le oscure sue porte,
l'arco di Stige sei, l'ombra di sera, il fiato di notte,
la coltre triste, che in ultimo ci ricopre;
nero, colore dispensier di Morte.

Rosso, oh tu, fra i colori, il piú giovane,
per te si dilegua, in fuga si pone malinconia;
colore delle corolle fragranti, di labbra accese,
tu l'anima sei dei sensi, oh colore terrestre!

Azzurro, mite, puro che i cieli dischiudi
vestigia di angeli, letto del mare: la tua nobiltà
sorride serena nelle stelle dei fiordalisi
(tu, caro, ad Enrico di Ofterdingen, emblema).

Translated by Carlo L. Golino

Rhyme from the Confino

I ran all night along the river
sighing that dawn should be now
and no one be in my company
(only my own silence, my own tears);
and I prayed that, all anger spent,
my shadow might disappear into the night
and they should look elsewhere for blood and prey
the guards who, instead, searched only for me.

Colors

Black: you are Black Hell, its dark portals,
the arch of Styx, the shadow of evening, the breath of night,
the dismal quilt that lastly shrouds our bodies;
black, color and bestower of Death.

Red, you of all colors are the youngest,
before you all sadness fades away and is put to flight;
color of fragrant blooms, of burning lips,
you are the soul of the senses, oh earthly color!

Blue, gentle, pure, you disclose the heavens;
vestige of angels, bed of the sea: your nobility
smiles serene within the stars of the fleurs-de-lis
(beloved emblem of Heinrich von Ofterdingen).

LUIGI BARTOLINI

Verde, color di pace pei campi, di mattina:
sopra te riposarmi, verde speranza, vorrei;
errare, ancora una volta alle tue luci e tue ombre,
cupo verde dei boschi di saggine chiaro verde.

Viola, trapasso d'ore, seduzione dell'infinito;
di doppia vita partecipi, alle albe e ai tramonti;
colore delle nuvole, e di Roma, da Monte Mario,
colore delle distanze e degli attutiti clamori.

Giallo, allegria, infedeltà, colore dell'Oriente,
stole trapunte d'oro, vesti d'odalische, sole;
esuberanti distese di grani maturi fra i tulipani;
ma la tua vita è breve, oh colore senza soste!

Bianco, o tu solitario, o tu amico,
tutto nascondi dietro l'immobile viso,
colore della Sfinge; celata, dalle tue ali, la sorte
nostra ultima tu già conosci, silenzioso, impenetrabile.

Green, color of peaceful fields, in the morning:
I should like to rest upon you, green hope;
wander again within your lights, within your shadows,
dark green of the woods, bright green of sorghum.

Violet, passage of hours, lure of the infinite;
you enjoy a double life, at dawn and at sunset;
color of the clouds, of Rome, from Monte Mario,
color of distances and of hushed clamors.

Yellow, merriment, infidelity, color of the Orient,
stoles quilted in gold, dress of odalisques, rays of sun;
exuberant expanses of ripe wheat among the tulips;
but your life is brief, O color without respite!

White, solitary, friendly color,
you hide all behind your motionless visage,
color of the Sphynx; silent, impenetrable, you know
already our final fate, concealed within your wings.

CARLO BETOCCHI

Alla sorella

Gli aghi dei pini tremolanti, e un sole
di fanciullezza con inerme cuore
vaní per la campagna,
fu piccolo, poi nulla. Una farfalla

oggi vola sui mirti. Infanzia torna,
a girotondo la piccola gonna
danzante; ahi, come neve
bevuta ai monti è dall'azzurro lieve.

Quel tuo volto piú macero, quel tuo
soffrire, e l'esser madre, e nell'oscuro
giacinto odor dell'ombra
lo sfuggir del tuo sguardo, che asseconda

la mia tristezza: credi tu che mai
piú noi saremo felici? Io vedo mari
ininterrotti a sponda
di questa breve vita; io vedo l'onda

già verde, l'alba, e l'isola che perde
la sua tristezza, e l'alte cime accende
a un sol che non tramonta;
vedo tra i rami, e sembra si nascondano,

i trattenuti pianti che tu ami,
stormi d'uccelli di sui campi grami

Translated by Carlo L. Golino

To His Sister

Quivering pine needles, a sun
of childhood with harmless heart
vanished through the countryside,
became small, then nothing. A butterfly

today skims over the myrtle. Infancy returns,
its little skirt dancing in a ring;
alas, like snow drunk
on mountain tops by the airy sky.

Your face more gaunt, your sorrow,
your being a mother and, in the dark
hyacinth scent of the shade,
your evasive glances favor

my sadness: do you think that ever
again we shall be happy? I see
endless oceans as the shore of this
our brief life; I see the wave

already green, the dawn, and the island
its sadness lost, its highest peaks lit
by a sun that does not set;
I see among the branches, seemingly in hiding,

the suppressed tears that you love,
I see black myriads of bright

della terrestre sera,
splendidi e in dubbio la miriade nera.

Un dolce pomeriggio d'inverno

« *L'eterno corpo dell'uomo
è l'immaginazione* ».
W. BLAKE

Un dolce pomeriggio d'inverno, dolce
perché la luce non era piú che una cosa
immutabile, non alba né tramonto,
i miei pensieri svanirono come molte
farfalle, nei giardini pieni di rose
che vivono di là, fuori del mondo.

Come povere farfalle, come quelle
semplici di primavera che sugli orti
volano innumerevoli gialle e bianche,
ecco se ne andavan via leggiere e belle
ecco inseguivano i miei occhi assorti,
sempre piú in alto volavano mai stanche.

Tutte le forme diventavan farfalle
intanto, non c'era piú una cosa ferma
intorno a me, una tremolante luce
d'un altro mondo invadeva quella valle
dove io fuggivo, e con la sua voce eterna
cantava l'angelo che a Te mi conduce.

uncertain birds, flocking over
the barren fields of the earth's evening.

On a Mild Winter Afternoon

*"The eternal body of man
is the imagination."*
             W. BLAKE

On a mild winter afternoon, mild
because the light had become a thing
immutable, neither dawn nor twilight,
my thoughts like so many butterflies
vanished in the garden full of roses
that live beyond, outside the world.

Like poor butterflies, like those common ones
of springtime that numberless,
yellow and white, fly through the gardens,
so they flew away light and fair
as they pursued my rapt eyes,
never tiring, higher and higher.

All shapes became as butterflies
meanwhile, nothing kept its stillness
around me, a quivering light
from other worlds filled the valley
where I fled, and with eternal voice
sang the angel that leads me to You.

CESARE PAVESE

Estate

C'è un giardino chiaro, fra mura basse,
di erba secca e di luce, che cuoce adagio
la sua terra. È una luce che sa di mare.
Tu respiri quell'erba. Tocchi i capelli
e ne scuoti il ricordo.

                          Ho veduto cadere
molti frutti, dolci, su un'erba che so,
con un tonfo. Così trasalisci tu pure
al sussulto del sangue. Tu muovi il capo
come intorno accadesse un prodigio d'aria
e il prodigio sei tu. C'è un sapore uguale
nei tuoi occhi e nel caldo ricordo.

                                     Ascolti.
Le parole che ascolti ti toccano appena.
Hai nel viso calmo un pensiero chiaro
che ti finge alle spalle la luce del mare.
Hai nel viso un silenzio che preme il cuore
con un tonfo, e ne stilla una pena antica
come il succo dei frutti caduti allora.

La terra e la morte

Hai viso di pietra scolpita,
sangue di terra dura,

Translated by Norman T. Di Giovanni

Summer

There is a bright garden between low walls,
with dry grass and with light slowly baking
its earth. A radiance with the flavor of the sea.
You breathe that grass. You touch your hair,
shaking off its memory.

                         I have seen
the ripe fruit fall on familiar grass,
with a dull sound. So you too start
at the leap of your blood. You turn your head
as if a marvel of air took place around you
and the marvel is you. The same savor
is in your eyes and in the warm memory.

                                  You listen.
The words that you hear scarcely touch you.
On your calm face is a bright thought
that dissembles the sea's radiance at your back.
Your face has a silence that strikes the heart
with a dull sound, pressing from it ancient sorrows
like the juice of fruit just fallen.

The Earth and Death

You have a face of carved stone,
blood like the unyielding land,

sei venuta dal mare.
Tutto accogli e scruti
e respingi da te
come il mare. Nel cuore
hai silenzio, hai parole
inghiottite. Sei buia.
Per te l'alba è silenzio.

E sei come le voci
della terra — l'urto
della secchia nel pozzo,
la canzone del fuoco,
il tonfo di una mela;
le parole rassegnate
e cupe sulle soglie,
il grido del bimbo—le cose
che non passano mai.
Tu non muti. Sei buia.

Sei la cantina chiusa,
dal battuto di terra,
dov'è entrato una volta
ch'era scalzo il bambino,
e ci ripensa sempre.
Sei la camera buia
cui si ripensa sempre,
come al cortile antico
dove s'apriva l'alba.

. . . .
. . . .
. . . .

E allora noi vili
che amavamo la sera
bisbigliante, le case,
i sentieri sul fiume,
le luci rosse e sporche

you came from the sea.
And all that you gather and probe
you cast away
as does the sea. In your heart
you hold silence, you hold
swallowed words. You are dark.
For you the dawn is silence.

And you are like the voices
of the land—the plunge
of the bucket in the well,
the song of the fire,
the thud of an apple;
words across thresholds,
sullen and resigned;
an infant's cry—things
that never pass on.
You do not change. You are dark.

You are the wine cellar,
sealed by a layer of earth
which the barefoot child
once entered,
and forever recalls.
You are the dark room
one forever recalls,
like the ancient courtyard
where the dawn unfolded.

. . . .
. . . .
. . . .

And then we cowards
who once loved the whispering
evening, the houses,
the paths along the river,
the red and dirty lights

di quei luoghi, il dolore
addolcito e taciuto —
noi strappammo le mani
dalla viva catena
e tacemmo, ma il cuore
ci sussultò di sangue,
e non fu piú dolcezza,
non fu piú abbandonarsi
al sentiero sul fiume —
— non piú servi, sapemmo
di essere soli e vivi.

Sei la terra e la morte.
La tua stagione è il buio
e il silenzio. Non vive
cosa che piú di te
sia remota dall'alba.

Quando sembri destarti
sei soltanto dolore,
l'hai negli occhi e nel sangue
ma tu non senti. Vivi
come vive una pietra,
come la terra dura.
E ti vestono sogni
movimenti singulti
che tu ignori. Il dolore
come l'acqua di un lago
trepida e ti circonda.
Sono cerchi sull'acqua.
Tu li lasci svanire.
Sei la terra e la morte.

of those places, the sorrow
made sweet and secret—
we tore our hands
from the living chains
and were silent, but our hearts
rushed with blood.
It was no longer sweetness,
no longer surrendering ourselves
to the path along the river—
—slaves no more, we learned
we were alone, alive.

You are the earth and death.
Your season is darkness
and silence. Nothing
alive is more remote
from dawn than you.

When you verge on waking
you are only pain,
you hold it in your eyes and blood
but you do not feel. You live
as a stone lives,
as the harsh earth.
You are clothed in dreams
in gestures, in sobs
of which you're unaware. Pain
like the waters of a lake
trembles and encircles you.
They are rings on the water.
You let them fade.
The earth you are, and death.

ATTILIO BERTOLUCCI

Amore

La luna coronata di margherite
Ride nei vaghi occhi infermi,
Caprioli d'argento
Scherzano nelle radure del cielo.

I fiori si macchiano di sangue...
Oh lontana, lontana, in questa notte,
Come una nave con le sue vele
Nel mare scuro...

Ma presto verrà il tempo
Arido e melodioso dei papaveri,
E tu sarai tornata
Già donna.

La notte d'ottobre

Mi ha svegliato il tuo canto solitario
Triste amica dell'ottobre, innocente civetta
Era la notte,
Brulicante di sogni come api.

Ronzavano
Agitando le chiome di fuoco

Translated by Carlo L. Golino

Love

The moon crowned by daisies
Smiles within your weak pretty eyes,
Silver roebucks
Play in the heavens' glades.

The flowers are stained with blood . . .
Oh far, far away, through the night,
Like a ship with its sails
On the dark sea . . .

But soon the time of poppies,
Dry, melodious will come,
And you will have returned
A woman now.

October Night

Your lonely song awoke me
Melancholy October friend, innocent owl,
It was night,
Swarming with dreams as with bees.

They hummed
Shaking their fiery hair

E le bionde barbe,
Ma i loro occhi erano rossi e tristi.

Tu cantavi, malinconica
Come una prigioniera orientale,
Sotto il cielo azzurro...
Io ascoltavo battere il mio cuore.

Inverno

Inverno, gracili sogni
Sforiscono sugli origlieri,
Giardini lontani fra nebbie
Nella pianura che sfuma
In mezzo alle luci dell'alba.
Voci come in un ricordo
D'infanzia, prigioniere del gelo,
S'allontanano verso la campagna;
Ninfe dagli occhi dolci e chiari
Fra gli alberi spogli, sotto il cielo grigio,
Cacciatori che attraversano un ruscello,
Mentre uno stormo d'uccelli s'alza a volo.

Là in fondo quella casa
Che ospitale appare,
Coperta di bianco,
In un silenzio da fiaba.

E attraverso i vetri
Si vede la fiamma rossa
Nel caminetto vacillare.
I treni arrivano,
È domenica, è Natale?
Più non scende lieve
Sulla terra la neve.

And their blond beards,
But their eyes were red and sad.

You were singing, melancholy
As an oriental prisoner,
Under the blue sky . . .
I listened to the beating of my heart.

Winter

Winter, feeble dreams
Wilting on the pillow,
Faraway gardens in the mists
Of vanishing plains
Amid the light of dawn.
Voices as in a childhood
Memory fade into the countryside,
Prisoners of the frost,
Nymphs with gentle, light eyes
Among the bare trees, under grey skies,
Hunters crossing over a brook,
While a flock of birds rises in flight.

Down there a house
Looking hospitable,
Covered with white,
In fairy-story silence.

And through the panes,
Wavering in the hearth
The glowing flames.
Trains arrive,
Is it Sunday, perhaps Christmas?
No longer does the snow, white
Upon the ground, fall light.

SANDRO PENNA

★

La veneta piazzetta
antica e mesta, accoglie
odor di mare. E voli
di colombi. Ma resta
nella memoria — e incanta
di sé la luce — il volo
del giovane ciclista
vòlto all'amico: un soffio
melodico: « Vai solo? »

★

I pini solitari lungo il mare
desolato non sanno del mio amore.
Li sveglia il vento, la pioggia
dolce li bacia, il tuono
lontano li addormenta.
Ma i pini solitari non sapranno
mai del mio amore, mai della mia gioia.

Amore della terra, colma gioia
incompresa. Oh dove porti
lontano! Un giorno
i pini solitari non vedranno

Translated by Carlo L. Golino

★

The little Venetian square
mournful and ancient, gathers
the fragrance of the sea. And flights
of pigeons. But memory
retains—bewitching
the very light—the flying
young cyclist
turning to his friend: a melodious
whisper: "Going alone?"

★

The solitary pines along the desolate
sea do not know of my love.
The wind awakens them, sweet
the rain kisses them, the thunder
from afar lulls them to sleep.
But the solitary pines will never
know of my love, will never know my joy.

Love of the earth, an overflowing joy
not understood. Oh where so far away
do you lead! Some day
the solitary pines will never see

— la pioggia li lecca, il sole li addormenta —
coll'amore danzare la mia morte.

★

Il mio amore è furtivo
come quello di un povero.
Ognuno può rubarlo.
Ed io dovrò lasciarlo.

Per ciò, fiume silente,
per ciò, mio dolce colle,
io non posso chiamarlo
amor semplicemente.

Ma tu, colle dorato,
e tu, mio fiume molle,
sapete che il mio amore
davvero è un grande amore.

Il pericolo odiato
per adesso non c'è?
Ma voi sapete, amici,
che nel mio cuore è.

Piangere mi vedrete,
o voi sempre felici,
non come piango già,
non di felicità.

★

La luna di settembre su la buia
valle addormenta ai contadini il canto.

—the rain licks them, the sun lulls them to sleep—
love dancing together with my death.

★

Stealthy is my love
like a poor man's love.
Anyone can steal it.
And I shall have to leave it.

And so, my silent river,
And so, my mellow hill,
I cannot simply call it
love and nothing more.

But you, O golden hill,
and you, my languid river,
you do know my love
is truly a great love.

The hated danger
is not yet upon me?
But you know well, my friends,
that in my heart it be.

Weeping you will see me,
you, forever happy,
not tears I now confess,
not tears of happiness.

★

The September moon over the dark valley
lulls to sleep the peasant's song.

Una cadenza insiste: come lento
respiro di animale, nel silenzio,
salpa la valle se la luna sale.

Altro respira qui, dolce animale
anch'egli silenzioso. Ma un tumulto
di vita in me ripete antica vita.

Più vivo di così non sarò mai.

Passando sopra un ponte
alto sull'imbrunire
guardando l'orizzonte
ti pare di svanire.

Ma la campagna resta
piena di cose vere
e tante azzurre sfere
non valgono una festa.

A rhythm persists: much like an animal's
slow breathing, in the silence,
the valley seems to float as the moon rises.

Someone else is breathing here, he too a gentle
silent animal. But life's turmoil
within me again stirs ancient life.

I shall never again be more alive.

Passing over a high bridge
gazing at approaching night
over the horizon's ridge
is like vanishing in flight.

But all the fields stay
full of all things real
and all the spheres ethereal
aren't worth one holiday.

IV

HERMETIC POETS

GIUSEPPE UNGARETTI

Agonia

Morire come allodole assetate
sul miraggio

O come quaglia
passato il mare
nei primi cespugli
perchè di volare
non ha più voglia

Ma non vivere di lamento
come un cardellino accecato

In memoria

Si chiamava
Moammed Sceab

Discendente
di emiri di nomadi
suicida
perchè non aveva più
Patria

Amò la Francia
e mutò nome

Translated by Lowry Nelson, Jr.

Dying

To die like thirsting larks
before a mirage

Or like the quail
having crossed the sea
in the first branches
because it has lost
all desire to fly

But not to live on anguish
like a blinded finch

In Memoriam

His name
was Mohammed Sheab

Scion
of emirs of nomads
a suicide
because he had
no country

He loved France
and changed his name

GIUSEPPE UNGARETTI

Fu Marcel
ma non era Francese
e non sapeva più
vivere
nella tenda dei suoi
dove si ascolta la cantilena
del Corano
gustando un caffè

E non sapeva
sciogliere
il canto
del suo abbandono

L'ho accompagnato
insieme alla padrona dell'albergo
dove abitavamo
a Parigi
dal numero 5 della rue des Carmes
appassito vicolo in discesa

Riposa
nel camposanto d'Ivry
sobborgo che pare
sempre
in una giornata
di una
decomposta fiera

E forse io solo
so ancora
che visse

Sono una creatura

Come questa pietra
del S. Michele

He became Marcel
but he was not French
and could no longer
dwell
in his people's tent
where they listen
to the Koran sing-song
sipping coffee

He could no longer
intone
the song
of his abandonment

With the woman who owned the hotel
I followed him
from where we lived
in Paris
down from number 5 rue des Carmes
a faded sloping little street

He rests
in the graveyard at Ivry
a suburb that seems
always
on the day
of a dismantled
fair

And perhaps I alone
still know
that he had lived

I Am a Creature

Like this rock
of San Michele

così fredda
così dura
così prosciugata
così refrattaria
così totalmente
disanimata

Come questa pietra
è il mio pianto
che non si vede

La morte
si sconta
vivendo

I fiumi

Mi tengo a quest'albero mutilato
abbandonato in questa dolina
che ha il languore
di un circo
prima o dopo lo spettacolo
e guardo
il passaggio quieto
delle nuvole sulla luna

Stamani mi sono disteso
in un'urna d'acqua
e come una reliquia
ho riposato

L'Isonzo scorrendo
mi levigava
come un suo sasso

Ho tirato su
le mie quattr'ossa

so cold
so hard
so desiccated
so impervious
so utterly
unspirited

Like this rock
are my tears
you cannot see

Death
we redeem
by living

Rivers

I cling to this mangled tree
left to lie in the crevasse
that has all the indolence
of a circus
before or after the show
and I watch
the tranquil passing
of clouds across the moon

This morning I stretched out
in an urn of water
and like a relic
rested

The Isonzo rushing
polished me
as one of its stones

I pulled
my bones together

e me ne sono andato
come un acrobata
sull'acqua

Mi sono accoccolato
vicino ai miei panni
sudici di guerra
e come un beduino
mi sono chinato a ricevere
il sole

Questo è l'Isonzo
e qui meglio
mi sono riconosciuto
una docile fibra
dell'universo

Il mio supplizio
è quando
non mi credo
in armonia

Ma quelle occulte
mani
che m'intridono
mi regalano
la rara
felicità

Ho ripassato
le epoche
della mia vita

Questi sono
i miei fiumi

Questo è il Serchio
al quale hanno attinto

and off I went
on the water
like an acrobat

I squatted down
beside my clothes
grimy with war
and like a Bedouin
I bowed to receive
the sun

This is the Isonzo
and there I best
acknowledged myself
a pliant fiber
in the universe

My torment
comes when
I think myself
out of harmony

But those hidden
hands
that immerse me
give me freely
an uncommon
happiness

I have gone
through the stages
of my life

These are my rivers

This is the Serchio
from which perhaps two thousand years

duemil'anni forse
di gente mia campagnola
e mio padre e mia madre

Questo è il Nilo
che mi ha visto
nascere e crescere
e ardere d'inconsapevolezza
nelle estese pianure

Questa è la Senna
e in quel suo torbido
mi sono rimescolato
e mi sono conosciuto

Questi sono i miei fiumi
contati nell'Isonzo

Questa è la mia nostalgia
che in ognuno
mi traspare
ora ch'è notte
che la mia vita mi pare
una corolla
di tenebre

L'isola

A una proda ove sera era perenne
Di anziane selve assorte, scese,
E s'inoltrò
E lo richiamò rumore di penne
Ch'erasi sciolto dallo stridulo
Batticuore dell'acqua torrida,
E una larva (languiva
E rifioriva) vide;

of my own country folk
and my father and my mother
have drawn their water

This is the Nile
that saw me born
and saw me grow
and burn in unawareness
on the expansive plains

This is the Seine
and in that swirl
I mingled
and I came to know myself

These are my rivers
tallied in the Isonzo

This is my nostalgia
that in each of them
it comes to me
now that night has fallen
that my life to me seems
a flower
of shadows

The Island

To a shore where ancient brooding woods
Made perpetual evening, he descended,
And walked forth,
And, lured by rustling of feathers
Perceptible above the shrill
Heart-throbbing of the torrid waters,
He saw, as it drooped
and rose again, a ghost;

Ritornato a salire vide
Ch'era una ninfa e dormiva
Ritta abbracciata a un olmo.

In sé da simulacro a fiamma vera
Errando, giunse a un prato ove
l'ombra negli occhi s'addensava
Delle vergini come
Sera appiè degli ulivi;
Distillavano i rami
Una pioggia pigra di dardi,
Qua pecore s'erano appisolate
Sotto il liscio tepore,
Altre brucavano
La coltre luminosa;
Le mani del pastore erano un vetro
Levigato di fioca febbre.

La pietà

1

Sono un uomo ferito.

E me ne vorrei andare
E finalmente giungere,
Pietà, dove si ascolta
L'uomo che è solo con sé.

Non ho che superbia e bontà.

E mi sento esiliato in mezzo agli uomini.

Ma per essi sto in pena.

Non sarei degno di tornare in me?

Ho popolato di nomi il silenzio.

Ho fatto a pezzi cuore e mente
Per cadere in servitù di parole?

Turning to ascend he saw
It was a nymph sleeping upright,
Her arms around an elm.

Wandering inwardly from image
To real flame, he came upon a meadow where
The shadows in the eyes of maidens gathered
Like evening at the foot of olive trees;
The branches distilled
An indolent rain of darts;
Here sheep had lain down to nap
Under the bland warmth;
Others browsed
On the gleaming cover;
The shepherd's hands were glass
Smoothened by faint fever.

Pity

1

I am a wounded man.

I would like to set out
And finally reach the place,
Pity, where the man alone
With himself can be heard.

I have nothing but pride and goodness.

And I feel in exile among men.

But it is for them that I suffer.

Could I be unworthy to return to myself?

I have peopled the silence with names.

Have I shattered my heart and mind
Only to fall a slave to words?

Regno sopra fantasmi.

O foglie secche,
Anima portata qua e là...

No, odio il vento e la sua voce
di bestia immemorabile.

Dio, coloro che t'implorano
Non ti conoscono più che di nome?

M'hai discacciato dalla vita.

Mi discaccerai dalla morte?

Forse l'uomo è anche indegno di sperare.

Anche la fonte del rimorso è secca?

Il peccato che importa,
Se alla purezza non conduce più.

La carne si ricorda appena
Che una volta fu forte.

È folle e usata, l'anima.

Dio, guarda la nostra debolezza.

Vorremmo una certezza.

Di noi nemmeno più ridi?

E compiangici dunque, crudeltà.

Non ne posso più di stare murato
Nel desiderio senza amore.

Una traccia mostraci di giustizia.

La tua legge qual è?

Fulmina le mie povere emozioni,
Liberami dall'inquietudine.

Sono stanco di urlare senza voce.

I reign over phantoms.

O withered leaves,
Soul borne hither and yon . . .

No, I hate the wind with its voice
Like an immemorial beast.

Do those, God, who implore you
Know you now by name alone?

You have driven me from life.

Will you drive me now from death?

Man is perhaps unworthy even of hope.

Has even the fountain of remorse gone dry?

What use is sin
If it can no longer make us pure?

Flesh barely remembers
That it once was strong.

The soul is mad and worn.

God, look upon our weakness.

We would have some certainty.

Do you now not even laugh at us?

Cruelty, then, pity us.

I can no longer stand to be walled up
In this desire without love.

Show us a single trace of justice.

Which, then, is your law?

Shatter my poor passions,
Free me from disquietude.

I am tired of wailing voicelessly.

2

Malinconiosa carne
Dove una volta pullulò la gioia,
Occhi socchiusi del risveglio stanco,
Tu vedi, anima troppo matura,
Quel che sarò, caduto nella terra?

È nei vivi la strada dei defunti,

Siamo noi la fiumana d'ombre,

Sono esse il grano che ci scoppia in sogno,

Loro è la lontananza che ci resta,

E loro è l'ombra che dà peso ai nomi.

La speranza d'un mucchio d'ombra
E null'altro è la nostra sorte?

E tu non saresti che un sogno, Dio?

Almeno un sogno, temerari,
Vogliamo ti somigli.

È parto della demenza più chiara.

Non trema in nuvole di rami
Come passeri di mattina
Al filo delle palpebre.

In noi sta e langue, piaga misteriosa.

3

La luce che ci punge
È un filo sempre più sottile.

Più non abbagli tu, se non uccidi?

Dammi questa gioia suprema.

2

Melancholy flesh
Where once joy teemed,
Half-open eyes in weary awakening,
Can you see, soul all-too-ripe,
What I shall become when fallen on earth?

The path of the dead is in the living,

It is we who are the river of wraiths,

It is they who are the seed bursting in our dreams,

Theirs is the distance that remains for us,

And theirs is the shadow that gives weight to names.

Is then our lot no other
Than hoping for a mass of shadow?

And are you, God, perhaps no more than a dream?

Rashly, we want at least
A dream to resemble you.

It is the fruit of utter madness.

It does not tremble in clouds of branches
Like sparrows in the morning
On the edge of eyelids.

It is fixed and lingering in us, a mysterious wound.

3

The light that pierces us
Is an ever thinner thread.

Will you no longer dazzle unless you kill?

Give me that highest joy.

4

L'uomo, monotono universo,
Crede allargarsi i beni
E dalle sue mani febbrili
Non escono senza fine che limiti.

Attaccato sul vuoto
Al suo filo di ragno,
Non teme e non seduce
Se non il proprio grido.

Ripara il logorio alzando tombe,
E per pensarti, Eterno,
Non ha che le bestemmie.

Tu ti spezzasti

1

I molti, immani, sparsi, grigi sassi
Frementi ancora alle segrete fionde
Di originarie fiamme soffocate
Od ai terrori di fiumane vergini
Ruinanti in inplacabili carezze,
— Sopra l'abbaglio della sabbia rigidi
In un vuoto orizzonte, non rammenti?

E la recline, che s'apriva all'unico
Raccogliersi dell'ombra nella valle,
Araucaria, anelando ingigantita,
Volta nell'ardua selce d'erme fibre
Più delle altre dannate refrattaria,
Fresca la bocca di farfalle e d'erbe,
Dove dalle radici si tagliava,
— Non la rammenti delirante muta
Sopra tre palmi d'un rotondo ciottolo
In un perfetto bilico
Magicamente apparsa?

4

Man, a monotonous universe,
Thinks to increase his goods
But from his feverish hands
Come nothing more than endless boundaries.

Clinging over the void
To this spider thread,
He fears and lures nothing
Unless his own outcry.

Decay he repairs by building tombs,
And to think of you, the Eternal,
He has only blasphemies.

You Were Shattered

1

Those many giant, grey and scattered stones
Still shaking from the secret slings
Of primal flames now quenched
Or from the fears that virgin rivers brought
Crashing down in their implacable embrace
—Rigid in the glitter of the sand
On a blank horizon, you remember?

And leaning, opening toward the only
Mass of shadow in the valley,
Yearning, magnified, the Araucaria pine,
Curling into the hard flint with lonely veins
More stubborn than those other accursed,
Its mouth fresh with butterflies and grass
Where severed from its roots,
—Do you remember it, incoherent, dumb,
On a few feet of rounded rock
In perfect balance,
Magically there?

Di ramo in ramo fiorrancino lieve,
Ebbri di meraviglia gli avidi occhi
Ne conquistavi la screziata cima,
Temerario, musico bimbo,
Solo per rivedere all'imo lucido
D'un fondo e quieto baratro di mare
Favolose testuggini
Ridestarsi fra l'alghe.

Della natura estrema la tensione
E le subacquee pompe,
Funebri moniti.

2

Alzavi le braccia come ali
E ridavi nascita al vento
Correndo nel peso dell'aria immota.
Nessuno mai vide posare
Il tuo lieve piede di danza.

3

Grazia felice,
Non avresti potuto non spezzarti
In una cecità tanto indurita
Tu semplice soffio e cristallo,

Troppo umano lampo per l'empio,
Selvoso, accanito, ronzante
Ruggito d'un sole ignudo.

From branch to branch light kinglet,
Your eager eyes drunk with wonder,
You conquered its dappled peak,
Rash, melodious child,
Just to see once more in the lucid depths
Of a profound and tranquil ocean abyss
Fabulous tortoises
Roused from sleep among the seaweed.

Tension of nature in extremes
And underwater pageants,
Funereal admonitions.

2

You raised your arms like wings
And rendered birth to the wind,
Running in the weight of the motionless air.
No one ever saw linger
Your light and dancing feet.

3

Fortunate grace,
You could not help but shatter
In a blindness so hardened—
And you simple breath and glass,

Too human a flash for the pagan,
Sylvan, relentless, droning
Roar of a naked sun.

*Cori descrittivi di stati d'animo
di Didone*
da *La Terra Promessa*

1

Dileguandosi l'ombra,

In lontananza d'anni,

Quando non laceravano gli affanni,

L'allora, odi, puerile
Petto eregersi bramato
E l'occhio tuo allarmato
Fuoco incauto svelare dell'aprile
Da un'odorosa gota.

Scherno, spettro solerte
Che rendi il tempo inerte
E lungamente la sua furia nota:

Il cuore roso, sgombra:

Ma potrà, mute lotte
sopite, dileguarsi da età, notte?

2

La sera si prolunga
Per un sospeso fuoco
E un fremito nell'erba a poco a poco
Pare infinito a sorte ricongiunga.

Lunare allora inavvertita nacque
Eco, e si fuse al brivido dell'acque.

Non so chi fu più vivo,
Il sussurrio sino all'ebbro rivo
O l'attenta che tenera si tacque.

Choruses Descriptive of Dido's States of Mind

(from *The Promised Land*)

1

The shadow fading

In distance of years

When worries did not maim,

Your then (hear me) childish
Breast rising desired
And your eye from fears
Revealing reckless fire
Of April from a fragrant cheek.

Mockery, vigilant phantom,
You who make inoperative time
And lengthily its fury known.

The gnawed heart, disengage!

But, night, silent struggles
Lulled, can it fade from age?

2

Evening is prolonged
By a hanging fire
And a quiver among the plants
Slowly seems an infinite return to fate.

Unnoticed lunar Echo then
Was born and melted in the shuddering of waves.

I know not which was more alive,
The murmuring up to the giddy stream
Or the hearkener who gently hushed.

EUGENIO MONTALE

Falsetto

Esterina, i vent'anni ti minacciano,
grigiorosea nube
che a poco a poco in sé ti chiude.
Ciò intendi e non paventi.
Sommersa ti vedremo
nella fumèa che il vento
lacera o addensa, violento.
Poi dal fiotto di cenere uscirai
adusta piú che mai,
proteso a un'avventura piú lontana
l'intento viso che assembra
l'arciera Diana.
Salgono i venti autunni,
t'avviluppano andate primavere;
ecco per te rintocca
un presagio nell'elisie sfere.
Un suono non ti renda
qual d'incrinata brocca
percossa! io prego sia
per te concerto ineffabile
di sonagliere.

La dubbia dimane non t'impaura.
Leggiadra ti distendi
sullo scoglio lucente di sale
e al sole bruci le membra.

Translated by Carlo L. Golino

Falsetto

Esterina, your twenty years threaten you,
pink and grey cloud
slowly enclosing you within its folds.
This you know and do not fear.
We behold you submerged
in the smoky vapor that the wind
violently lifts away or thickens.
Then from the wave of ashes you'll emerge
more than ever scorched,
turning toward more distant adventures
your rapt features that resemble
the huntress Diana.
The twenty autumns rise,
past springtimes enfold you;
And now for you an omen
tolls in the Elysian spheres.
Let it not be the sound
of a cracked jug
struck! I pray
that it may be for you a concert
of ineffable little bells.

The doubtful future does not frighten you.
Graceful you stretch out
on a shining salty reef
and in the sun you bronze your limbs,

Ricordi la lucertola
ferma sul masso brullo;
te insidia giovinezza,
quella il lacciòlo d'erba del fanciullo.
L'acqua è la forza che ti tempra,
nell'acqua ti ritrovi e ti rinnovi:
noi ti pensiamo come un'alga, un ciottolo,
come un'equorea creatura
che la salsedine non intacca
ma torna al lito piú pura.

Hai ben ragione tu! Non turbare
di ubbie il sorridente presente.
La tua gaiezza impegna già il futuro
ed un crollar di spalle
dirocca i fortilizî
del tuo domani oscuro.
T'alzi e t'avanzi sul ponticello
esiguo, sopra il gorgo che stride:
il tuo profilo s'incide
contro uno sfondo di perla.
Esiti a sommo del tremulo asse,
poi ridi, e come spiccata da un vento
t'abbatti fra le braccia
del tuo divino amico che t'afferra.

Ti guardiamo noi, della razza
di chi rimane a terra.

Dora Markus

I

Fu dove il ponte di legno
mette a porto Corsini sul mare alto
e rari uomini, quasi immoti, calano
o salpano le reti. Con un segno

recalling the lizard
motionless on the naked boulder;
you by youth are threatened,
he by the boy's grass noose.
Water is the strength that tempers you
in the water you find and renew yourself;
we think of you as an alga, a pebble,
as an ocean creature
uncorroded by brine
who returns purer to the shore.

How right you are! Do not cloud
with doubts the smiling present.
Your gaiety already binds the future
and a shrug of the shoulders
lays waste the citadels
of your dark tomorrow.
You rise, advance upon the slender board,
above the whirlpool of roaring waters:
your profile is chiseled
against a background of pearl.
At the edge of the shaky plank you hesitate,
then laugh, and as if plucked by wind
you cast yourself into the arms
of your divine friend who seizes you.

We watch you,
we of the earth-bound race.

Dora Markus

I

It was where the wooden pier
juts into the sea at Porto Corsini
and a few men, barely moving, lower
or raise their nets. A gesture

della mano additavi all'altra sponda
invisibile la tua patria vera.
Poi seguimmo il canale fino alla darsena
della città, lucida di fuliggine,
nella bassura dove s'affondava
una primavera inerte, senza memoria.

E qui dove un'antica vita
si screzia in una dolce
ansietà d'Oriente,
le tue parole iridavano come le scaglie
della triglia moribonda.

La tua irrequietudine mi fa pensare
agli uccelli di passo che urtano ai fari
nelle sere tempestose:
è una tempesta anche la tua dolcezza,
turbina e non appare,
e i suoi riposi sono anche piú rari.
Non so come stremata tu resisti
in questo lago
d'indifferenza ch'è il tuo cuore; forse
ti salva un amuleto che tu tieni
vicino alla matita delle labbra,
al piumino, alla lima: un topo bianco
d'avorio; e cosí esisti!

II

Ormai nella tua Carinzia
di mirti fioriti e di stagni,
china sul bordo sorvegli
la carpa che timida abbocca
o segui sui tigli, tra gl'irti
pinnacoli le accensioni
del vespro e nell'acque un avvampo
di tende da scali e pensioni.

of your hand pointed on the other shore,
invisible, to your true native land.
Then we followed the canal into the city
as far as the docks, shiny with soot,
in that flat land where an inert spring
was sinking, void of memory.

And here where an ancient life
speckles into a mild
anxiety from the Orient,
your words, like the scales on a dying fish,
flashed into rainbow.

Your restlessness brings to mind
birds of passage that on stormy evenings
strike against the lighthouse;
even your sweetness is but a storm
that swirls below the surface,
its pauses even more rare.
I know not how, exhausted, you survive
in this sea of indifference
that is your heart; perhaps
what saves you is the amulet you keep
beside your powder puff,
the lipstick, the file: a white mouse,
of ivory; and thus you exist!

II

Now in Carinthia, your land
of flowering myrtles and ponds,
bending over the edge you watch
the carp timidly biting,
or above the lime trees, among the ragged
pinnacles you follow the early lights
of evening, and on the water a flash
of awnings from the quays and lodging-houses.

La sera che si protende
sull'umida conca non porta
col palpito dei motori
che gemiti d'oche e un interno
di nivee maioliche dice
allo specchio annerito che ti vide
diversa una storia di errori
imperturbati e la incide
dove la spugna non giunge.

La tua leggenda, Dora!
Ma è scritta già in quegli sguardi
di uomini che hanno fedine
altere e deboli in grandi
ritratti d'oro e ritorna
ad ogni accordo che esprime
l'armonica guasta nell'ora
che abbuia, sempre piú tardi.

È scritta là. Il sempreverde
alloro per la cucina
resiste, la voce non muta,
Ravenna è lontana, distilla
veleno una fede feroce.
Che vuole da te? Non si cede
voce, leggenda o destino....
Ma è tardi, sempre piú tardi.

La casa dei doganieri

Tu non ricordi la casa dei doganieri
sul rialzo a strapiombo sulla scogliera:
desolata t'attende dalla sera
in cui v'entrò lo sciame dei tuoi pensieri
e vi sostò irrequieto.

The evening that looms
over the humid basin carries
along with the throb of motors
only the cries of geese, and an interior
of snow-white tiles
tells the blackened mirror
that knew you formerly a story
of calm mistakes, engraving it there
where the sponge does not reach.

Your legend, Dora!
It is already written in the glances
of men with proud
thin whiskers in large
gilded portraits, and recurs
with every chord played
by the broken harmonica in the hours
when it grows dark still later and later.

It is written there. The evergreen
laurel for the kitchen
survives, the voice unchanged,
Ravenna is far; ferocious
faith distills the venom.
What does it want of you? One does not yield
voice, legend or destiny . . .
But it is late, always later.

The Customs-House

You don't remember the customs-house
jutting over rocks from the height:
desolate it awaits you since the night
when into it your thoughts came swarming
and there remained, restless, pausing.

Libeccio sferza da anni le vecchie mura
e il suono del tuo riso non è piú lieto:
la bussola va impazzita all'avventura
e il calcolo dei dadi piú non torna.
Tu non ricordi; altro tempo frastorna
la tua memoria; un filo s'addipana.

Ne tengo ancora un capo; ma s'allontana
la casa e in cima al tetto la banderuola
affumicata gira senza pietà.
Ne tengo un capo; ma tu resti sola
né qui respiri nell'oscurità.

Oh l'orizzonte in fuga, dove s'accende
rara la luce della petroliera!
Il varco è qui? (Ripullula il frangente
ancora sulla balza che scoscende...)
Tu non ricordi la casa di questa
mia sera. Ed io non so chi va e chi resta.

Sotto la pioggia

Un murmure; e la tua casa s'appanna
come nella bruma del ricordo
e lacrima la palma ora che sordo
preme il disfacimento che ritiene
nell'afa delle serre anche le nude
speranze ed il pensiero che rimorde.

« Per amor de la fiebre » ... mi conduce
un vortice con te. Raggia vermiglia
una tenda, una finestra si rinchiude.
Sulla rampa materna ora cammina,
guscio d'uovo che va tra la fanghiglia,
poca vita tra sbatter d'ombra e luce.

For years Libeccio has lashed the ancient walls
and your laughter's sound is no longer gay:
the compass madly turns whichever way,
the dice are thrown but the guess is wrong.
You don't remember; your memory is bound
to other times; a thread is wound.

I still retain one end; but the house
grows distant and the blackened vane
upon its roofs relentlessly spins.
I retain one end; but you remain alone
nor do you breathe here in the darkness.

Oh the fleeting horizon, where seldom
the tanker's lights are lit!
Is this the pass? (The breakers crash again
against the slope of the crumbling heights . . .)
You don't remember the house of this, my evening.
And I know not who stays and who is leaving.

Under the Rain

A murmur; and your house grows dim
as in the winter solstice of remembrance
and so the palm weeps, for relentless
presses the decay that holds
within the sultriness of the greenhouse
even bare hopes and remorseful thoughts.

"Per amor de la fiebre" . . . I am carried
into a whirlpool with you. A bright red awning
gleams, a window is closed.
On the maternal slope go walking,
like an eggshell lost in the mire,
bits of life betwixt shade and light.

Strideva Adiós muchachos, compañeros
de mi vida, il tuo disco dalla corte:
e m'è cara la maschera se ancora
di là dal mulinello della sorte
mi rimane il sobbalzo che riporta
al tuo sentiero.
Seguo i lucidi strosci e in fondo, a nembi,
il fumo strascicato d'una nave.
Si punteggia uno squarcio...
        Per te intendo
ciò che osa la cicogna quando alzato
il volo dalla cuspide nebbiosa
rémiga verso la Città del Capo.

Eastbourne

« Dio salvi il Re » intonano le trombe
da un padiglione erto su palafitte
che aprono il varco al mare quando sale
a distruggere peste
umide di cavalli nella sabbia
del litorale.

Freddo un vento m'investe
ma un guizzo accende i vetri
e il candore di mica delle rupi
ne risplende.

Bank Holiday.... Riporta l'onda lunga
della mia vita
a striscio, troppo dolce sulla china.
Si fa tardi. I fragori si distendono,
si chiudono in sordina.

Vanno su sedie a ruote i mutilati,
li accompagnano cani dagli orecchi

From the courtyard *Adiós muchachos
compañeros de mi vida* screeched your record:
and dear to me still is the mask
if beyond the whirlwind of fate I am left
with the jolt that leads me back
upon your path.
I follow bright downpours, and beyond, drifting
puffs of smoke from a ship.
A gash of light appears . . .
                              Because of you
I understand the daring stork
when rising into flight from foggy peaks
he wings his way toward Capetown.

Eastbourne

"God save the King" the trumpets sound
from the pavilion high upon the piles
that open the way for a rising sea
to erase hoofmarks
of horses still fresh upon
the sandy shore.

A cold wind assails me
but soon a flash lights up the windows
and the candor of the mica cliffs
reflects their brilliance.

Bank Holiday . . . it brings back the long wave
of my life,
grazing, too gentle upon its lapse.
It grows late. The rumbling sounds scatter
dying into a muted hush.

On their wheelchairs invalids go by,
they have as company long-eared dogs,

lunghi, bimbi in silenzio o vecchi. (Forse
domani tutto parrà un sogno).
                              E vieni
tu pure voce prigioniera, sciolta
anima ch'è smarrita,
voce di sangue, persa e restituita
alla mia sera.

Come lucente muove sui suoi spicchi
la porta di un albergo
— risponde un'altra e le rivolge un raggio —
m'agita un carosello che travolge
tutto dentro il suo giro; ed io in ascolto
(« mia patria! ») riconosco il tuo respiro,
anch'io mi levo e il giorno è troppo folto.

Tutto apparirà vano: anche la forza
che nella sua tenace ganga aggrega
i vivi e i morti, gli alberi e gli scogli
e si svolge da te, per te. La festa
non ha pietà. Rimanda
il suo scroscio la banda, si dispiega
nel primo buio una bontà senz'armi.

Vince il male... La ruota non s'arresta.

Anche tu lo sapevi, luce-in-tenebra.

Nella plaga che brucia, dove sei
scomparsa al primo tocco delle campane, solo
rimane l'acre tizzo che già fu
Bank Holiday.

or silent children, or aged men. (Perhaps
tomorrow all will seem a dream.)
                              You also come
captive voice, freed soul
that has gone astray,
voice of blood, lost and restored
to this my evening.

As bright upon its wings revolves
a hotel door
—another with a gleam replies—
so I am stirred by a carousel of feelings
that sweeps all away within its whirl; and listening
("my country") I recognize your breathing,
I too arise and the day is all too dense.

All will seem vain; even the strength
that with tenacious hold together binds
the living and the dead, the trees and reefs
and by you moved, for you moves. The holiday
has no mercy. Again the band
sends forth its crashing sound, in the dusk
an unguarded goodness unfolds.

Evil conquers . . . The wheel will not be stopped.

You also knew it, light-in-darkness.

In the burning land where
you vanished at the bell's first stroke,
alone remains the bitter ember, once
Bank Holiday.

Notizie dall'Amiata

Il fuoco d'artifizio del maltempo
sarà murmure d'araie a tarda sera.
La stanza ha travature
tarlate ed un sentore di meloni
penetra dall'assito. Le fumate
morbide che risalgono una valle
d'elfi e di funghi fino al cono diafano
della cima m'intorbidano i vetri,
e ti scrivo di qui, da questo tavolo
remoto, dalla cellula di miele
di una sfera lanciata nello spazio —
e le gabbie coperte, il focolare
dove i marroni esplodono, le vene
di salnitro e di muffa sono il quadro
dove tra poco romperai. La vita
che t'affàbula è ancora troppo breve
se ti contiene! Schiude la tua icona
il fondo luminoso. Fuori piove.

* * *

E tu seguissi le fragili architetture
annerite dal tempo e dal carbone,
i cortili quadrati che hanno nel mezzo
il pozzo profondissimo; tu seguissi
il volo infagottato degli uccelli
notturni e in fondo al borro l'allucciolío
della Galassia, la fascia d'ogni tormento.
Ma il passo che risuona a lungo nell'oscuro
è di chi va solitario e altro non vede
che questo cadere di archi, di ombre e di pieghe.
Le stelle hanno trapunti troppo sottili,
l'occhio del campanile è fermo sulle due ore,
i rampicanti anch'essi sono un'ascesa
di tenebre ed il loro profumo duole amaro.
Ritorna domani piú freddo, vento del nord,
spezza le antiche mani dell'arenaria,

News from Amiata

The fireworks of inclement weather
will be the beehives' murmur at the evening's close.
The room has worm-eaten beams
and the scent of melons
seeps through the wooden planks. Smoky wisps
rising softly over a valley
of elves and mushrooms up to the peak's
transparent cone, becloud my windows,
and I write to you from here, from this remote
table, from the honey cell
of a sphere launched into space—
and the covered cages, the hearth
where chestnuts burst, the veins
of niter and mold are the frame
into which you will soon emerge. The life
that bewitches you is still too short
if it can encompass you: The bright background
reveals your ikon. Outside it rains.

* * *

And were you to follow the fragile architecture
blackened by time and coal,
the square courtyards where in the center
is the deep, deep well; were you to follow
the huddled flight of birds
of night and in the gully's depth the glitter
of the Galaxy, to every wound a dressing.
But the long echoing step in the dark
belongs to the lonely walker who sees only
this falling drapery of arches, shadows, folds.
The stars are too subtly quilted,
the tower's eye is fixed at two o'clock,
even the climbing plants are an ascent
of shadows and theirs an aching, bitter scent.
Return tomorrow colder, wind of the north,
shatter the sandstone's ancient hands,

sconvolgi i libri d'ore nei solai,
e tutto sia lente tranquilla, dominio, prigione
del senso che non dispera! Ritorna piú forte
vento di settentrione che rendi care
le catene e suggelli le spore del possibile!
Son troppo strette le strade, gli asini neri
che zoccolano in fila dànno scintille,
dal picco nascosto rispondono vampate di magnesio.
Oh il gocciolío che scende a rilento
dalle casipole buie, il tempo fatto acqua,
il lungo colloquio coi poveri morti, la cenere, il vento,
il vento che tarda, la morte, la morte che vive!

* * *

Questa rissa cristiana che non ha
se non parole d'ombra e di lamento
che ti porta di me? Meno di quanto
t'ha rapito la gora che s'interra
dolce nella sua chiusa di cemento.
Una ruota di mola, un vecchio tronco,
confini ultimi al mondo. Si disfà
un cumulo di strame: e tardi usciti
a unire la mia veglia al tuo profondo
sonno che li riceve, i porcospini
s'abbeverano a un filo di pietà.

L'arca

La tempesta di primavera ha sconvolto
l'ombrello del salice,
al turbine d'aprile
s'è impigliato nell'orto il vello d'oro
che nasconde i miei morti,
i miei cani fidati, le mie vecchie
serve — quanti da allora
(quando il salce era biondo e io ne stroncavo

derange the books of hours in the attics,
and let it all be a tranquil lens, power, prison
of undespairing sense. Return, now stronger,
wind from the north. You make our chains dear to us
and seal the spores of what is possible.
Too narrow are the roads; the black asses,
clattering in single file, strike sparks;
from hidden peaks magnesium flares reply.
Ah, the dripping trickle that slowly drops
from darkest hovels, time made water,
the long dialogue with the poor dead, the ash, the wind,
the delaying wind, and death, death that lives!

* * *

This Christian fray that has only
words of shadow, of lament,
what does it bring from me to you? Less than what
the flume, burrowing gently along
its cement walls, has torn away from you.
A millstone wheel, an ancient trunk:
final boundaries to the world. A heap of straw
decays; and late appearing,
to bind my vigil to your deep
sleep that welcomes them, the porcupines
drink from a thread of pity.

The Ark

The springtime storm upset
the willow's crown,
the April whirlwind
entangled in the kitchen garden
the golden fleece that hides my dead,
my faithful dogs, my old
maidservants—those who since
(when blond was the willow and with my sling

le anella con la fionda) son calati,
vivi, nel trabocchetto. La tempesta
certo li riunirà sotto quel tetto
di prima, ma lontano, piú lontano
di questa terra folgorata dove
bollono calce e sangue nell'impronta
del piede umano. Fuma il ramaiolo
in cucina, un suo tondo di riflessi
accentra i volti ossuti, i musi aguzzi
e li protegge in fondo la magnolia
se un soffio ve la getta. La tempesta
primaverile scuote d'un latrato
di fedeltà la mia arca, o perduti.

Giorno e notte

Anche una piuma che vola può disegnare
la tua figura, o il raggio che gioca a rimpiattino
tra i mobili, il rimando dello specchio
di un bambino, dai tetti. Sul giro delle mura
strascichi di vapore prolungano le guglie
dei pioppi e giú sul trespolo s'arruffa il pappagallo
dell'arrotino. Poi la notte afosa
sulla piazzola, e i passi, e sempre questa dura
fatica di affondare per risorgere eguali
da secoli, o da istanti, d'incubo che non possono
ritrovare la luce dei tuoi occhi nell'antro
incandescente — e ancora le stesse grida e i lunghi
pianti sulla veranda
se rimbomba improvviso il colpo che t'arrossa
la gola e schianta l'ali o perigliosa
annunziatrice dell'alba
e si destano i chiostri e gli ospedali
a un lacerío di trombe...

I tore its curls) have sunk
still alive, into the pitfall. Surely the storm
will reunite them under the roof
of old, but far away, farther away
beyond this bolt-struck land where
lime and blood seethe in the footprints
of mankind. The ladle smokes
in the kitchen, its round reflections
center the bony faces, the pointed muzzles
and in the background the magnolia shields them
if a gust should fling it. The springtime
storm shakes with a bark
of faithfulness my ark, oh lost ones.

Day and Night

Even a floating feather in the air can trace
your shape, or the sunbeam that plays hide-and-seek
among the furniture, the reflection of a child's mirror
from the roofs. Above the circle of the city walls
lingering streams of vapor lengthen the spires
of the poplar trees and down below the knife-grinder's parrot
ruffles its feathers on the trestle. Then the stifling night
on the small square, and the footsteps, and as always
this harsh struggle of sinking to rise again unchanged
for centuries, for moments, from nightmares
that cannot find again the light of your eyes
in the glowing cave—and still the same cries, the long
weeping on the verandah
if suddenly the shot resounds that reddens
your throat and shatters your wings, you perilous
harbinger of the dawn
and the cloisters and the hospitals awake
at the rending blasts of trumpets. . . .

L'anguilla

L'anguilla, la sirena
dei mari freddi che lascia il Baltico
per giungere ai nostri mari,
ai nostri estuari, ai fiumi
che risale in profondo, sotto la piena avversa,
di ramo in ramo e poi
di capello in capello, assottigliati,
sempre più addentro, sempre più nel cuore
del macigno, filtrando
tra gorielli di melma finché un giorno
una luce seccata dai castagni
ne accende il guizzo in pozze d'acquamorta,
nei fossi che congiungono
i balzi dell'Appennino alla Romagna;
l'anguilla, torcia, frusta,
freccia d'Amore in terra
che solo i nostri botri o i disseccati
ruscelli pirenaici riconducono
a paradisi di fecondazione;
l'anima verde che cerca
vita dove là solo
morde l'arsura e la desolazione,
la scintilla che dice
tutto comincia quando tutto pare
incarbonirsi, bronco seppellito,
l'iride breve gemella
di quella che incastoni in mezzo ai cigli
e fai brillare intatta in mezzo ai figli
dell'uomo, immersi nel tuo fango, puoi tu
non crederla sorella?

The Eel

The eel, the siren
of cold seas that leaves the Baltic
to reach our seas,
our estuaries, our rivers
where it swims upstream down deep against the adverse tides,
from branch to branch and then
from fine to finer stem,
penetrating still further into the boulder's
core, filtering
through miry channels till one day
a light striking through the chestnut trees
kindles its darting leap in stagnant pools,
in the ditches that connect
the Apennine cliffs to Romagna;
the eel, torch, whip,
arrow of Love on earth
that only our gullies or arid
pyrenean brooks bring back
to heavens of fertility;
the green soul that seeks
life there where only
drought and desolation gnaw,
the spark that says
all things begin when all things seem
burning to coals, buried stump,
the brief rainbow, twin sister
of the one you set between your lashes
and let shine intact among the sons
of man, immersed in your mire, can you
believe that she is not your sister?

LIBERO DE LIBERO

La mia notte ciociara

È una casa in Patrica Ciociara:
finestre per i monti e quel fiacco limone
dice ancora parole di foglie
alla secca stagione di Cacume.

Anche stanotte sono stato lassù
per labili tunnel, in punta di piedi:
lassù seduto ho atteso la civetta,
forse andata con qualche messaggio
dove al fiume Sacco la valle si consola.
Sotto voce io cerco perduti compagni di gesta,
Aurelio, Netto, e Federigo, acerbi fantasmi
di gatti vaganti tra i cancelli della Loia,
Mammattina, vetusta nutrice di garofani
e l'acqua fuggiasca per la stretta, i cari orti.

Lassù il cielo è una compatta foglia,
nervature cocenti, e a volte raminga
la luna, corno sfiatato che tenta un richiamo.
Trepidi passi di persone ascolto
mai stanche di aprire e chiudere porte,
il vento delle vesti continua a frusciare
per le stanze, convegno di sedie ormai.

La mia notte ciociara scalpita talora
di segreti cavalli, boschi in agguato,

Translated by Carlo L. Golino

*My Ciociara Night**

There is a house in Patrica Ciociara:
with windows to the mountains and a weary lemon tree
that with its leaves continues still to speak
to Cacume's withered, dry season.

Even tonight I have been up there
through slippery tunnels, walking on tiptoe:
sitting, I awaited the screech owl,
who was gone perhaps with a message
to where the valley in the Sacco is consoled.
I seek in whispers the lost companions of my exploits,
Aurelio, Netto, and Federigo, the embittered ghosts
of cats roaming through the Loia's gates,
Mammattina, the ancient nurse of carnations
and the water fleeting through the narrows, the beloved gardens.

Up there the sky is a compact leaf,
with burning veins, and the moon at times
wanders by, a breathless horn striving for a call.
I listen to the anxious steps of people
who never tire of closing, opening doors
the rustling wind of gowns still lingers
in the rooms, where only chairs gather now.

My Ciociara night at times resounds
with pawings of secret horses, woods lying in wait,

* Ciociara from Ciociaria, the native region of the poet, between Rome and Naples.

LIBERO DE LIBERO

e so chi sei tu che mi scuote con fragile tosse
e so che la tua lenta carrozza nel buio
si scioglie con lagrimose fiammelle:
penso alla pioggia e non ti salva il mantello
dal freddo e l'orecchio tu pieghi al vento,
postiglione loquace ti narra crudeli fatti.
Tu dici che sono un debole uomo,
capace di singhiozzi quando mi pesi
sulla spalla come un addio: non è facile
piangere per te che hai deciso di sparire.

La mia notte ciociara è sempre un frizzante odore
latte che s'arriccia alle malve corrotte,
un gaudioso fuoco di strugli, e quella rupe
all'ombra grassa d'un cipresso, paese dilaniato.
La mia notte ciociara è una storia funesta:
anniversari eterni di bimbi rapiti,
di giovinette che non furono donne,
uomini partiti con l'inverno, un mattino,
senza bagagli e qualcosa da dire.
A Patrica l'alba è tutta un rosicchiare
di topi che fanno buchi lucenti nelle fratte,
e si sgretola un giorno stantio di castani.

I know who you are with frail cough shaking me
and I know that your slow carriage in the darkness
vanishes in the midst of tearful little flames.
I think of the rain and of your cloak, a vain shield
against the cold, you cock your ear into the wind,
a garrulous coachman recounts cruel deeds.
You say that I am a weak man,
capable of sobs when on my shoulder
you weigh like a farewell: it is not easy
to weep for you, who have decided to depart.

My Ciociara night is always a sharp scent
milk curling on decaying mallows,
a joyous bonfire, and that rock
in the thick shadow of a cypress, a lacerated land.
My Ciociara night is a sorrowful tale:
eternal anniversaries of enraptured children,
of girls that were never women,
of men that departed with the winter, one morning,
without baggage or a word to say.
At Patrica the dawn is all a nibbling
of mice that gnaw bright holes in the hedges,
and the day crumbles away, stale, amid the chestnut trees.

ALFONSO GATTO

Erba e latte

Mansueta di campani, la sera remota
alle finestre pallide di cielo
odora umido, e tace in gradini la casa vuota.
Svanisce, continuo tepore di gelo,

nella bottiglia verde, il latte: nuvole chiare
lontanano nel fioco armonioso tacere
della campagna. Sembra compiuto nel limitare
della mia casa il sonno delle riviere.

Beato vòlto al sereno, quasi la notte m'apra
continuamente a sgorgare in fragranza.
Tepida e lieve, cauta, mi lambisce una capra:
odora d'erba e di muschio la stanza.

Morto ai paesi

Bambino festoso incontro alla strada
del giorno chiamato lungamente
sarò morto nel gioco dei paesi:
prima che la sera cada
porta a porta si sente
la quiete fresca del mare, stormire.

Translated by John A. Scott

Grass and Milk

The distant evening peaceful with the sound of bells
at the windows pale with heaven
smells damp, and the empty house is silent in its steps.
The milk, with a constant glow of ice,

vanishes in the green bottle: pale clouds
are wafted in the frail harmonious silence
of the countryside. The sleep of great rivers
seems fulfilled in the threshold of my home.

Rapt face toward the clear vault, as if the night
opens me out in gushing fragrance.
A goat carefully laps me with her tongue, warm and light:
the room is filled with the fragrance of grass and moss.

Dead in the Villages

Happy child facing the road
of yearned-for day
I shall be dead in the play of villages:
before evening falls
from door to door is heard
the cool calm of the sea, murmuring.

Il bambino festoso dove muore
nel suo grido fa sera
e nel silenzio trova bianco odore
di madre, la leggera
sembianza del suo volto.

Resta vergogna calda sulla fronte,
a rare
voci ritorna
lungo le porte ad ascoltare
il paese cantato sui carri.

Piangerà chi non piange

Con tutti i morti scende nella sera,
con tutta l'ombra dell'infanzia il lume
di casa in casa, e anche il mare è solo.
Piangerà chi non piange piangerà...

Dentro la pioggia le carrozze nere,
la bambina dei fiori stringe i gridi
chiusi nel petto e le parole morte.
Piangerà chi non piange piangerà...

Nelle case dementi la paura
veste di seta azzurra le fanciulle
innammorate con la luna al piede.
Piangerà chi non piange piangerà...

I saraceni ridono anneriti
al taglio secco delle bocche, nenie
tristi dai denti colano appassite
come un vino di petali. Son morte,
affondate sull'orma d'altri morti,
le vecchie al fondo delle case e il bianco
mare degli anni fissano sparendo.

The happy child dying
brings nightfall in his cry
and in the silence he finds the white fragrance
of a mother, the light
semblance of her face.

Burning shame remains on the brow,
he returns
along the doorways to listen
to the village song on the carts
in few
voices.

Weep—Those Whose Eyes Are Dry Shall Weep

The evening light accompanied by all the dead
and the whole shadow of childhood descends slowly
from house to house, and the sea too is alone.
Weep—those whose eyes are dry shall weep . . .

The black cabs in the rain,
the young flower-girl stifling the cries
locked in her breast and the dead utterances.
Weep—those whose eyes are dry shall weep . . .

In the house gone mad, fear
drapes blue silk about love-stricken girls
with the moon at their feet.
Weep—those whose eyes are dry shall weep . . .

The Saracens laugh with the black line
of their withered lips, while blighted lays
of sadness exude from their lips
like a wine of petals. The old women
in the depths of their houses are dead,
prostrate on the trail left by the deaths of others,
while, vanishing, they gaze on the white sea of time.

Oh, quel vuoto che resta è la spettrale
città dei vivi che improvvisa il cielo,
il suo cielo funesto, i suoi colori,
i frantumi d'un mondo che ci opprime.
Piangerà chi non piange piangerà...

Liberate la sera dai ricordi
delle donne di ferro che nei letti
affossano gli amanti e con le bocche
nere dei morti lasciano sui figli
la febbre i lumi i gridi, il brulichio
della vasta città ch'ebbe nel mare
l'urlo supremo della luce.   Annotta
sulle case in tumulto, e nel pensiero
l'ombra più della tenebra sprofonda
i fantasmi che parlano lontano
in tutto il mondo ove la luna è sola,
un canto in braccio ai venti e in cuore ai morti.

Piangerà chi non piange piangerà,
e la saggezza sconsolata è un sogno
che la speranza sia concessa all'uomo
come un ultimo pianto sulle cose.

Ah! the emptiness that remains is the ghostly
city of the living which conjures up the sky,
its mournful sky, its colors,
the wreckage of a world that oppresses us.
Weep—those whose eyes are dry shall weep . . .

Rid the evening of memories
of the iron women who gouge their lovers
in bed and with the black lips of the dead
leave upon their children
fever, lights, shouts, the swarming
mass of the vast city which found in the sea
the supreme cry of light.
       Night falls
upon the houses in turmoil, and in the mind
the shadows—more than the darkness—buries
the spirits which speak in the distance
over the whole earth where the moon is alone,
a song in the arms of the wind and in the hearts of the dead.

Weep—those whose eyes are dry shall weep,
and forlorn wisdom is a dream
that hope may be given to man
as a last lament on life.

MARIO LUZI

Avorio

Parla il cipresso equinoziale, oscuro
e montuoso esulta il capriolo,
dentro le fonti rosse le criniere
dai baci adagio lavan le cavalle.
Giú da foreste vaporose immensi
alle eccelse città battono i fiumi
lungamente, si muovono in un sogno
affettuose vele verso Olimpia.
Correranno le intense vie d'Oriente
ventilate fanciulle e dai mercati
salmastri guarderanno ilari il mondo.
Ma dove attingerò io la mia vita
ora che il tremebondo amore è morto?
Violavano le rose l'orizzonte,
esitanti città stavano in cielo
asperse di giardini tormentosi,
la sua voce nell'aria era una roccia
deserta e incolmabile di fiori.

Donna in Pisa

Non sempre fosti sola con me, spesso guardavi
lunghe feste appassite nei canali
scorrere sotto i ponti inseguite dal tempo,
tra i pampini, tra i prati languidi e il lume

Translated by Carlo L. Golino

Ivory

The equinoctial cypress speaks,
the dark mountain deer rejoices,
slowly the mares into red fountains
wash off kisses from their manes.
Down from the steamy forests to the lofty
cities immense rivers flow long on their
course, as in a dream caressing sails
set on their way toward Olympia.
They will ply the crowded routes of Orient,
wind-blown maids, and from the briny
markets they will look joyously upon the world.
But whence shall I draw my life
now that my trembling love is dead?
Roses once did violence to the horizon,
wavering cities were in the sky
strewn with tormenting gardens,
her voice in the air was a deserted crag
that flowers could never fill.

Woman in Pisa

Not always were you alone with me, often you watched
the long withered holidays flow
under the bridges in the canals pursued by time,
or among the tendrils, among the quiet meadows

della sera discendere i fondali
e le spire del fiume.

E talvolta era incerto tra noi chi fosse assente:
spesso vedevi i limpidi tornei
snodarsi nelle vie sotto i soli d'inverno,
tra logge, tra fiori fumidi e il gelo
delle mura sospingere i trofei
nella luce d'averno.

Donna altrimenti — e niente più simile alla vita —
calda d'impercettibili passioni
velata da un vapore di lagrime ideali
nel vento, sui ponti ultimi al fuoco
delle stelle apparivi dai portali,
dietro ai vetri di croco.

Vino e ocra

Piú lucente là esorbita la stella
di passione, piú amara sopra i fondachi
di perla in una nuvola acquiescente
la città dell'amata s'arrovella.

E ciascuno di voi sentitamente
solca il gelo d'un vento fatto inerme
alberi voi onde fu caro il marmo
nella serenità delle leggende.

Torna in cielo il sorriso, ma già eterna
la vedova di sé avvolge le tombe
per le campagne spente, un corno suona
le cacce sulle alture ove s'imperna

la luna. E voi tenere, voi auguste
essenze della vita! Nel tepore

and the evening light, you watched the river's depth
and its whirlpools vanish.

And at times I was not sure if you or I were absent:
often you saw the limpid tournaments
unwinding in the streets under winter suns,
among arches, damp and vaporous flowers and the cold
of the walls, driving their trophies
into the Avernian light.

A woman otherwise—and nothing that more resembles life—
warm with imperceptible passions
veiled by a vapor of ideal tears
in the wind, on the last bridges under the fiery
stars you appeared from the portals
behind the saffron panes.

Wine and Ocher

More brilliant there the star of passion
exceeds itself, bitterer still
above pearly warehouses my beloved's city
strives within an acquiescent cloud.

And each of you with sharpened senses
cuts through the cold of a wind made harmless:
trees you are, whence marble was endeared
in the serenity of legends.

The smile reappears in the sky, but already eternal
the widow in her fold wraps the tombs
through barren fields, a horn announces
the hunt over the hills where the moon

pivots. And you tender, you majestic
essences of life! In the warmth

dei lattici notturni esita il vento
cercandosi nel solco delle aduste

Orse d'un tempo. E là lungo invisibili
pianure e lo sfarzo dei torrenti
discorrono cavalli forsennati
e presso l'onda annusano le nuvole.

of the milky fragrances of night the wind pauses
seeking itself within the furrow of the burnt

Bears of yore. And there along invisible
plains and the splendor of torrents
frantic, discursive horses
sniff the clouds at the water's edge.

VITTORIO SERENI

3 Dicembre

All'ultimo tumulto dei binari
hai la tua pace, dove la città
in un volo di ponti e di viali
si getta alla campagna
e chi passa non sa
di te come tu non sai
degli echi delle cacce che ti sfiorano.

Pace forse è davvero la tua
e gli occhi che noi richiudemmo
per sempre ora riaperti
stupiscono
che ancora per noi
tu muoia un poco ogni anno
in questo giorno.

Terrazza

Improvvisa ci coglie la sera.
                          Piú non sai
dove il lago finisca;
un murmure soltanto
sfiora la nostra vita
sotto una pensile terrazza.

Translated by Carlo L. Golino

December 3

With a last roar upon the rails
you found your peace, where the city
in a flight of boulevards and bridges
leaps into the countryside
and the passer-by is unaware
of you as you are not aware
of the fleeting echoes of the hunt.

Yours perhaps is the true peace
and those, your eyes, we closed
for ever now reopened
wonder
that still for us
you die a little each year
upon this day.

The Terrace

Suddenly night overtakes us.
                           You no longer know
where the lake ends;
only a whisper
gently touches our life
under a hanging terrace.

Siamo tutti sospesi
a un tacito evento questa sera
entro quel raggio di torpediniera
che ci scruta poi gira se ne va.

Ma se tu manchi

Troppo il tempo ha tardato
per te d'essere detta
pena degli anni giovani.

Illividiva la città nel vento
o un'iride cadeva nella danza
dei riflessi beati:
eri nel ticchettio meditabondo
d'una sfera al mio polso
tra le pagine sfogliate
una marea di sole,
un'indolenza di sobborghi chiari
presto assunta in un volto
cosí a fondo scrutato,
ma un occhio lustro ma un tatto febbrile.

Venivano ombre leggere: — che porti
tu, che offri?... — Sorridevo
agli amici, svanivano
essi, svaniva
in tristezza la curva d'un viale.
Dietro ruote fuggite
smorzava i papaveri sui prati
una cinerea estate.

Ma se tu manchi
e anche il cielo è vinto
sono un barlume stento,
una voce superflua nel coro.

We hang suspenseful
from the silent event of this evening
within the searchlight of a torpedo boat
that peers at us then turns and disappears.

If You Are No Longer

Too long has time delayed
for you to be revealed
the sorrow of youthful years.

The city became livid in the wind
and a rainbow fell into the dance
of blissful reflections:
you were in the thoughtful ticking
of a circle on my wrist
among the turned pages
a flood of sunlight,
an indolence of bright suburbs
quickly drawn into a face
so thoroughly scanned,
but a shining eye, a feverish touch.

Light shadows came—what do you
bring, what do you offer? . . . —I smiled
at my friends,
they vanished, into sadness
vanished the bend upon the road.
Behind fleeting wheels
an ashen summer withered
the poppies in the meadows.

But if you no longer are
and even heaven is conquered
I am a stunted glimmer,
a voice superfluous in the choir.

V

SALVATORE QUASIMODO

—TOWARD TRANSITION

SALVATORE QUASIMODO

Vento a Tíndari

Tíndari, mite ti so
fra larghi colli pensile sull'acque
dell'isole dolci del dio,
oggi m'assali
e ti chini in cuore.

Salgo vertici aerei precipizi,
assorto al vento dei pini,
e la brigata che lieve m'accompagna
s'allontana nell'aria
onda di suoni e amore,
e tu mi prendi
da cui male mi trassi
e paure d'ombre e di silenzi,
rifugi di dolcezze un tempo assidue
e morte d'anima.

A te ignota è la terra
ove ogni giorno affondo
e segrete sillabe nutro:
altra luce ti sfoglia sopra i vetri
nella veste notturna,
e gioia non mia riposa
sul tuo grembo.

Aspro è l'esilio,
e la ricerca che chiudevo in te

Translations by Allen Mandelbaum

Wind at Tindari

Tindari, I know you mild
among broad hills, above the waters
of the god's soft islands,
today you assail me
and bend into my heart.

I climb peaks, airy precipices,
engulfed in the wind of the pines,
and my lighthearted company
moves far-off in air,
wave of sounds and love,
and you, beloved, take me,
you from whom I drew evil
and fears of shades and silences,
asylums of softness once assiduous
and death of soul.

To you unknown's the earth
wherein each day I sink
and nourish secret syllables:
other light unleafs you through your windows
in your nocturnal dress,
and joy not mine reposes
on your breast.

Harsh is exile,
and my search for harmony

d'armonia oggi si muta
in ansia precoce di morire;
e ogni amore è schermo alla tristezza,
tacito passo nel buio
dove mi hai posto
amaro pane a rompere.

Tíndari serena torna;
soave amico mi desta
che mi sporga nel cielo da una rupe
e io fingo timore a chi non sa
che vento profondo m'ha cercato.

Antico inverno

Desiderio delle tue mani chiare
nella penombra della fiamma:
sapevano di rovere e di rose;
di morte. Antico inverno.

Cercavano il miglio gli uccelli
ed erano súbito di neve;
cosí le parole.
Un po' di sole, una raggera d'angelo,
e poi la nebbia; e gli alberi,
e noi fatti d'aria al mattino.

Strada di Agrigentum

Là dura un vento che ricordo acceso
nelle criniere dei cavalli obliqui
in corsa lungo le pianure, vento
che macchia e rode l'arenaria e il cuore
dei telamoni lugubri, riversi

that was to end in you, alters today
into precocious dread of death:
and every love is a screen for sadness,
silent tread into the darkness
where you have set me
bitter bread to break.

Tindari, serene, return;
soft friend awaken me
that from a stone I thrust me skyward,
feigning fear to who knows not
what deep wind has sought me out.

Ancient Winter

Desire for your bright hands
in the penumbra of the flame:
they smelt of oak and roses;
of death. Ancient winter.

The birds were seeking grain
and suddenly were snowed under;
thus—words.
A little sun, an angel's glory,
and then the mist; and the trees
and us, made of air in the morning.

Street of Agrigentum

There a wind endures that I recall
kindled in the horses' manes, slanting
in races across the plains, a wind that stains
and wears away the sandstone and the heart
of mournful telamones, overturned

sopra l'erba. Anima antica, grigia
di rancori, torni a quel vento, annusi
il delicato muschio che riveste
i giganti sospinti giù dal cielo.
Come sola allo spazio che ti resta!
E più t'accori s'odi ancora il suono
che s'allontana largo verso il mare
dove Èspero già striscia mattutino:
il marranzano tristemente vibra
nella gola di carraio che risale
il colle nitido di luna, lento
tra il murmure d'ulivi saraceni.

Òboe sommerso

Avara pena, tarda il tuo dono
in questa mia ora
di sospirati abbandoni.

Un òboe gelido risillaba
gioia di foglie perenni,
non mie, e smemora;

in me si fa sera:
l'acqua tramonta
sulle mie mani erbose.

Ali oscillano in fioco cielo,
làbili: il cuore trasmigra
ed io son gerbido,

e i giorni una maceria.

on the grass. Ancient soul, now grey
with rancour, with this wind do you return
to sniff the delicate moss that cloaks the giants
downward thrust from heaven. How alone
you are within the space still left to you!
And more you grieve one hears again the sound
that moves far off and broadly towards the sea,
where Hesperus already creeps with morning:
the marranzano quivers sorrowfully
in the throat of the waggoner, who climbs
the hillside neat beneath the moonlight, slowly
amid the murmur of saracen olive trees.

Sunken Oboe

Miser pain, delay your gift
in this my hour
of longed-for abandons.

Chill, again an oboe utters
joy of everlasting leaves,
not mine, and disremembers;

in me, evening falls:
the water sets
on my grassy hands.

In a dim sky, fleeting
wings sway; the heart migrates
and I am fallow

and the days, rubble.

Di fresca donna riversa
in mezzo ai fiori

S'indovinava la stagione occulta
dall'ansia delle piogge notturne,
dal variar nei cieli delle nuvole,
ondose lievi culle;
ed ero morto.

Una città a mezz'aria sospesa
m'era ultimo esilio
e mi chiamavano intorno
le soavi donne d'un tempo,
e la madre fatta nuova dagli anni,
la dolce mano scegliendo dalle rose
con le piú bianche mi cingeva il capo.

Fuori era notte
e gli astri seguivano precisi
ignoti cammini in curve d'oro
e le cose fatte fuggitive
mi traevano in angoli segreti
per dirmi di giardini spalancati
e del senso di vita;
ma a me doleva ultimo sorriso

di fresca donna riversa in mezzo ai fiori.

Ed è subito sera

Ognuno sta solo sul cuor della terra
trafitto da un raggio di sole:
ed è subito sera.

Of Young Woman Bent Back Among the Flowers

One divined the occult season
from the anxiousness of nightly rains,
from clouds that varied in the skies,
wavy light cradles:
and I was dead.

A city hanging in mid-air
was my final exile,
around me called
the soft women of ago,
and, by years renewed, my mother
her gentle hand choosing roses,
with the whitest ones she garlanded my head.

Night outside,
in curves of gold, the stars pursued
precise and unknown paths
and things, made fugitive,
drew me to secret corners
to tell of gardens opened wide
and of the sense of life;
but I was grieved with the final smile

of young woman bent back among the flowers.

And Suddenly It's Evening

Each alone on the heart of the earth,
impaled upon a ray of sun:
and suddenly it's evening.

Imitazione della gioia

Dove gli alberi ancora
abbandonata piú fanno la sera,
come indolente
è svanito l'ultimo tuo passo,
che appare appena il fiore
sui tigli e insiste alla sua sorte.

Una ragione cerchi agli affetti,
provi il silenzio nella tua vita.
Altra ventura a me rivela
il tempo specchiato. Addolora
come la morte, bellezza ormai
in altri volti fulminea.
Perduto ho ogni cosa innocente,
anche in questa voce, superstite
a imitare la gioia.

Già la pioggia è con noi

Già la pioggia è con noi,
scuote l'aria silenziosa.
Le rondini sfiorano le acque spente
presso i laghetti lombardi,
volano come gabbiani sui piccoli pesci;
il fieno odora oltre i recinti degli orti.

Ancora un anno è bruciato,
senza un lamento, senza un grido
levato a vincere d'improvviso un giorno.

Imitation of Joy

Where the trees make evening
even more abandoned,
how languidly
your final step has vanished,
like the flower that scarce appears
on the linden, insistent on its fate.

You seek a motive for the feelings,
experience silence in your life.
Mirrored time reveals to me
a different destiny. Beauty flashing
now in other faces, saddens me
like death.
I have lost every innocent thing,
even in this voice, surviving
to imitate joy.

The Rain's Already With Us

The rain's already with us
tossing silent air.
The swallows skim spent waters
on the Lombard lakes,
fly like gulls at little fish;
beyond the garden enclosures, the scent of hay.

Again a year is burned,
without lament, without a cry
upraised to win us—suddenly—a day.

Davanti al simulacro d'Ilaria del Carretto

Sotto tenera luna già i tuoi colli,
lungo il Serchio fanciulle in vesti rosse
e turchine si muovono leggere.
Così al tuo dolce tempo, cara; e Sirio
perde colore, e ogni ora s'allontana,
e il gabbiano s'infuria sulle spiagge
derelitte. Gli amanti vanno lieti
nell'aria di settembre, i loro gesti
accompagnano ombre di parole
che conosci. Non hanno pietà; e tu
tenuta dalla terra, che lamenti?
Sei qui rimasta sola. Il mio sussulto
forse è il tuo, uguale d'ira e di spavento.
Remoti i morti e più ancora i vivi,
i miei compagni vili e taciturni.

Dalla rocca di Bergamo Alta

Hai udito il grido del gallo nell'aria
di là dalle murate, oltre le torri
gelide d'una luce che ignoravi,
grido fulmineo di vita, e stormire
di voci dentro le celle, e il richiamo
d'uccello della ronda avanti l'alba.
E non hai detto parole per te:
eri nel cerchio ormai di breve raggio:
e tacquero l'antilope e l'airone
persi in un soffio di fumo maligno,
talismani d'un mondo appena nato.
E passava la luna di febbraio
aperta sulla terra, ma a te forma
nella memoria, accesa al suo silenzio.
Anche tu fra i cipressi della Rocca
ora vai senza rumore; e qui l'ira

Before the Statue of Ilaria Del Caretto

Now your hills beneath a tender moon,
along the Serchio young girls
in red and turquoise dresses lightly move.
Thus, gentle one, in your sweet time;
and Sirius grows dim, each hour grows
more distant, and the seagull rages
on the derelict beaches. The lovers walk
lighthearted in the air of September, their gestures
accompany the shades of words
you recognize. They have no pity; and you,
held fast by earth, o what do you lament?
Here you remain alone. My shuddering
is yours perhaps: mine, too, with wrath and terror.
Remote the dead and even more the living,
my comrades vile and taciturn.

From the Fortress of Upper Bergamo

You have heard the cry of the cock in the air
beyond the ramparts, beyond the towers
chill with a light that you knew not,
lightning cry of life, and murmur
in the cells of voices and
the birdcall of the dawn patrol.
For yourself, you spoke no words:
you were in the narrow circle:
and the antelope and the heron stilled
lost in a gust of malignant smoke,
talismans of a world scarce born.
And the February moon did pass
plain upon the earth, for you
but a remembered form, alight in its silence.
You, too, among the cypresses
now soundless walk; and here the wrath

si quieta al verde dei giovani morti,
e la pietà lontana è quasi gioia.

Quasi un madrigale

Il girasole piega a occidente
e già precipita il giorno nel suo
occhio in rovina e l'aria dell'estate
s'addensa e già curva le foglie e il fumo
dei cantieri. S'allontana con scorrere
secco di nubi e stridere di fulmini
quest'ultimo gioco del cielo. Ancora,
e da anni, cara, ci ferma il mutarsi
degli alberi stretti dentro la cerchia
dei Navigli. Ma è sempre il nostro giorno
e sempre quel sole che se ne va
con il filo del suo raggio affettuoso.

Non ho piú ricordi, non voglio ricordare;
la memoria risale dalla morte,
la vita è senza fine. Ogni giorno
è nostro. Uno si fermerà per sempre,
e tu con me, quando ci sembri tardi.
Qui sull'argine del canale, i piedi
in altalena, come di fanciulli,
guardiamo l'acqua, i primi rami dentro
il suo colore verde che s'oscura.
E l'uomo che in silenzio s'avvicina
non nasconde il coltello fra le mani,
ma un fiore di geranio.

Lettera alla madre

"*Mater dulcissima*, ora scendono le nebbie,
il Naviglio urta confusamente sulle dighe,

is stilled in the green of the youthful dead
and the distant pity is almost joy.

Almost a Madrigal

The sunflower bends to the west, and day
already sets in its ruined eye,
the air of summer thickens, curves
the leaves, the smoke of the factories.
With the clouds' dry flow, the lightning's screech
this last game of the heavens moves
far-off. Again, love, as for years,
we pause at the changes in the trees
crowded in the circle of the canals.
But it is still our day, and still
that sun that takes its leave
with the thread of its affectionate ray.

I've no more memories, I do not want to remember;
memory rises up from death,
life is without end. Each day
is ours. One day will stop forever,
and you with me, when it seems late for us.
Here on the edge of the canal, our feet
swinging back-and-forth like children's,
let us watch the water, the first branches
in its darkening green.
And the man who approaches in silence
hides no knife within his hands,
but a geranium.

Letter to My Mother

"*Mater dulcissima*, now the mists descend,
the Naviglio dashes against its dikes,

gli alberi si gonfiano d'acqua, bruciano di neve;
non sono triste nel Nord: non sono
in pace con me, ma non aspetto
perdono da nessuno, molti mi devono lacrime
da uomo a uomo. So che non stai bene, che vivi
come tutte le madri dei poeti, povera
e giusta nella misura d'amore
per i figli lontani. Oggi sono io
che ti scrivo." — Finalmente, dirai, due parole
di quel ragazzo che fuggì di notte con un mantello corto
e alcuni versi in tasca. Povero, così pronto di cuore,
lo uccideranno un giorno in qualche luogo. —
"Certo, ricordo, fu da quel grigio scalo
di treni lenti che portavano mandorle e arance,
alla foce dell'Imera, il fiume pieno di gazze,
di sale, d'eucalyptus. Ma ora ti ringrazio,
questo voglio, dell'ironia che hai messo
sul mio labbro, mite come la tua.
Quel sorriso m'ha salvato da pianti e da dolori.
E non importa se ora ho qualche lacrima per te,
per tutti quelli che come te aspettano,
e non sanno che cosa. Ah, gentile morte,
non toccare l'orologio in cucina che batte sopra il muro
tutta la mia infanzia è passata sullo smalto
del suo quadrante, su quei fiori dipinti:
non toccare le mani, il cuore dei vecchi.
Ma forse qualcuno risponde? O morte di pietà,
morte di pudore. Addio, cara, addio, mia *dulcissima mater*."

the trees swell with water, burn with snow;
I am not sad in the North: I am not
at peace with myself, but I expect
pardon from no one, many owe me tears,
as man to man. I know you are not well, that you live
like all the mothers of poets, poor
and just in the measure of their love
for distant sons. Today it is I
who write to you." —At last, you will say, two words
from that boy who fled by night in a short coat,
a few lines in his pocket. Poor, so quick of heart,
one day they'll kill him somewhere.
"Surely, I remember, I left from that gray station
of slow trains that carried almonds and oranges,
at the mouth of the Imera, river full of magpies,
salt, of eucalyptus. But now I thank you—
this I would—for the irony you laid upon
my lips, mild as your own.
That smile has saved me from laments and griefs.
And it matters not if now I've some tears for you,
for all who wait—like you—
and know not what they wait. Ah, gentle death,
don't touch the clock in the kitchen that ticks on the wall;
all my childhood has passed on the enamel
of its face, upon those painted flowers:
don't touch the hands, the heart of the dead.
Perhaps someone will answer? O death of mercy,
death of modesty. Farewell, dear one, farewell, my
  dulcissima mater."

VI

NEW TRENDS

PIER PAOLO PASOLINI

L'Appennino

I

Teatro di dossi, ebbri, calcinati,
muto, è la muta luna che ti vive,
tiepida sulla Lucchesia dai prati

troppo umani, cocente sulle rive
della Versilia, così intera sul vuoto
del mare — attonita su stive,

carene, vele rattrappite, dopo
viaggi di vecchia, popolare pesca
tra l'Elba, l'Argentario...

La luna, non c'è altra vita che questa.
E vi si sbianca l'Italia da Pisa
sparsa sull'Arno in una morta festa

di luci, a Lucca, pudica nella grigia
luce della cattolica, superstite
sua perfezione...

Umana la luna da queste pietre
raggelate trae un calore
di alte passioni... È, dietro

il loro silenzio, il morto ardore
traspirato dalla muta origine:
il marmo, a Lucca o Pisa, il tufo

a Orvieto...

Translated by William F. Weaver

Apennine

I

Theatre of hilltops, drunken, lime-sown,
silent, the silent moon gives you life,
tender over Lucchesia, on the fields

that are all too human, burning
on Versilia's shore; so whole at the void
of the sea, the bemused moon on hulls,

in holds, wrinkled sails, after old,
folk fishing voyages between
Elba, the cape of Argentario . . .

The moon—there is no other life—
where Italy is whitened from Pisa,
strewn on the Arno in a dead festival

of lights, to Lucca, modest in the grey
light of its relic, Catholic
perfection . . .

The human moon from these chill
stones reflects the heat
of lofty passions, as if beyond

their silence a dead ardor
sweated from its silent origin;
marble at Lucca or Pisa, at Orvieto
sandstone . . .

II

                Non vi accende
la luna che grigiore, dove azzurri
gli etruschi dormono, non pende

che a udire voci di fanciulli
dai selciati di Pienza o di Tarquinia...
Sui dossi risuonanti, brulli

ricava in mezzo all'Appennino
Orvieto, stretto sul colle sospeso
tra campi arati da orefici, minia-

ture, e il cielo. Orvieto illeso
tra i secoli, pesto di mura e tetti
sui vicoli di terra, con l'esodo

del mulo tra pesti giovinetti
impastati nel tufo.

Chiusa nei nervi, nel lucido passo,
tra sgretolate muraglie e scoscese
case, la bestia sale su dal basso

con ai fianchi le tinozze d'accesa
uva, sotto il busto di Bonifacio
prossimo a farsi polvere, difeso

da barocca altezza nella medioevale
nicchia della muraglia.

III

È assente dal suo gesto Bonifacio,
dal reggere la fionda nella grossa
mano Davide, e Ilaria, solo Ilaria...

Dentro nel claustrale transetto
come dentro un acquario, son di marmo
rassegnato le palpebre, il petto

dove giunge le mani in una calma

II

                    The moon kindles
only greyness, where azure
Etruscans sleep; it only

bends to hear liturgical boys
from Pienza's cobbles or
Tarquinia's on the bare,

resounding hills from Apennines
it hollows out Orvieto, crowded
on the hill suspended over miniature

fields that goldsmiths plough, and the sky,
Orvieto, unharmed by centuries, pulp
of walls, roofs on earthen alleys, the mule's

exodus through pulp of youths
kneaded into the stone.

Closed in its nerves, its lucid gait,
between riven walls and tilting
houses, the mule climbs up from below

with baskets of flaming grapes
on his flanks, beneath the head
of Boniface, about to be dust, defended

by baroque loftiness in the wall's
medieval niche.

III

Boniface is absent from his gesture,
David's hand is heavy, holding
the sling, and Ilaria, only Ilaria . . .

Within the cloistered transept
as in an aquarium, her eyelids are
of resigned marble, her breast

where her hands join in calm,

lontananza. Lì c'è l'aurora
e la sera italiana, la sua grama

nascita, la sua morte incolore.
Sonno, i secoli vuoti: nessuno
scalpello potrà scalzare la mole

tenue di queste palpebre.

Jacopo con Ilaria scolpì l'Italia
perduta nella morte, quando
la sua età fu più pura e necessaria.

IV

Sotto le palpebre chiuse ride
tra i pidocchi il mammoccio di Cassino
comprato ai genitori; per le rive

furenti dell'Aniene, un assassino
e una puttana lo nutrono, nelle
coloniali notti in cui Ciampino

abbagliato sotto sbiadite stelle
vibra di aeroplani di regnanti,
e per i lungoteveri che sentinelle

del sesso battono in spossanti
attese intorno a terree latrine,
da San Paolo, a San Giovanni, ai canti

più caldi di Roma, si sentono supine
suonare le ore del mille
novecento cinquantuno, e s'incrina

la quiete, tra i tuguri e le basiliche.

Nelle chiuse palpebre d'Ilaria trema
l'infetta membrana delle notti
italiane... molle di brezza, serena

di luci... grida di giovanotti
caldi, ironici e sanguinari... odori

absent being. Here is Italy's dawn
and evening, its lean

birth, its dying without color.
Sleep, the hollow centuries; no scalpel
can lay bare the tender massiveness

of these eyelids.

Jacopo with Ilaria sculptured Italy,
lost in death, when her age
was more pure, more necessary.

IV

Beneath shut eyelids, among his
lice laughs the boy from Cassino,
sold by his parents, on the raging

banks of the Aniene, a killer
and a whore nurse him, through
the colonial nights when Ciampino

blinded with washed-out stars
hums with the airplanes of kings,
and along the boulevards, the beat

of sex's sentinels, in devastating
waits around the earthy latrines,
from San Paolo to San Giovanni, to

the hottest corners of Rome you hear
the supine hours of the night ringing
in nineteen fifty-one, there is a cracking

in the stillness, between basilicas and hovels.

In Ilaria's closed eyelids trembles
the infected membrane of Italian
nights . . . soft with breezes, calm

with lights . . . shouts of young people,
hot, ironic, bloody . . . smells

di stracci caldi, ora bagnati... motti

di vecchie voci meridionali... cori
emiliani leggeri tra borghi e maceri...
Dalla provincia viziosa ai cuori

bianchi dei globi dei bar salaci
delle periferie cittadine,
la carne e la miseria hanno placidi

ariosi suoni. Ma nelle veline
e massicce palpebre d'Ilaria, nulla
che non sia sonno. Forme mattutine

che, precoce, la morte alla fanciulla
legò al marmo. All'Italia non resta
che la sua morte marmorea, la brulla

sua gioventù interrotta...

Sotto le sue palpebre, nel suo
sonno, incarnata, la terra alla luna
ha un vergine orgasmo nell'argenteo buio

che sulla frana dell'Appennino sfuma
scosceso verso coste dove imperla
il Tirreno o l'Adriatico la spuma.

Dentro il rotondo recinto di pelli
e di metallo, isolato tra le fratte
in cerchio in una radura d'erba

verdissima sui dossi del Soratte,
dorme un umido, annerito gregge,
e il pastore con le membra contratte

nel calcare.

V

Sotto le sue palpebre chiuse Luni
all'addiaccio, e le trepide
città dove l'Appennino profuma

of hot rags, wet now . . . Quips

from old southern voices . . . choruses
from Emilia, weakened in ponds and villages.
From vice's province, in the white

hearts of the bulbs in dirty bars
in the suburbs of the city
flesh and poverty find placid,

airy sounds . . . and then? In the vellum
and massive eyelids of Ilaria, nothing
that is not sleep. Morning's shapes

that death, precocious, in this girl
bound to marble. Italy has nothing left
but her marble death, her barren,

interrupted youth . . .

Under her eyelids, in her sleep,
the earth, incarnate, in the moonlight
has a virgin transport in the silver

dark that on the landslip of the Apennine
declines, steep, toward coasts where
the Tyrrhenian and the Adriatic foam is pearled.

Within the round enclosure of skins
and metal, isolated among the thickets,
on a bare patch of grass, in a circle,

on the green, green slopes of Soracte,
sleeps a damp, sooty flock, and the shepherd,
his limbs all contracted

on the limestone.

V

Under those closed lids, Luni, like
a sheepfold, the fossil town,
and the timid cities where the Apennine

più umano nelle cesellate siepi,
tra i caldi arativi della Toscana,
o dove più selvaggio le vecchie pievi

assorbe nell'etrurio — s'allontanano
sull'ala dei vergini, chiari
suoni serali. Ed essa si dipana,

la catena, nei solchi secolari
delle vene del Serchio, dell'Ombrone
e, dietro rudi imbuti e terrei fari

d'albore, il Tevere, nel polverone
appenninico, pagano ancora...
Roma, dietro radure di peoni,

ruderi alessandrini e barocchi indora
alla luna, e disfatte borgate
irreligiose, dove tutto si ignora

che non sia sesso, grotte abitate
da feci e fanciulli; i lungofiumi
dal Pincio, all'Aventino, alle scarpate

dello spoglio San Paolo dove i lumi
ingialliscono la calda atmosfera,
risuonano dei passi che le umide

pietre macchiano, e la romana sera
echeggiandone, come una membrana
grattata da un vizioso dito, svela

più acuto l'odore dell'orina.

VI

Un esercito accampato nell'attesa
di farsi cristiano nella cristiana
città, occupa una marcita distesa

d'erba sozza nell'accesa campagna:
scendere anch'egli dentro la borghese
luce spera aspettando una umana

is perfume, more human in graven hedges,
among the warm arables of Tuscany,
or where more dead the unremembering parishes

are absorbed in Etruscan stone, in this old age
fade virginal, clear sounds
of evening. And it is unraveled—

the range, in the centuries' sillions,
the veins of the Serchio, the Ombrone
and, beyond the rough funnels and earthen beacons

of dawn, the Tiber, in the Apennine
dust-cloud, the Tiber pagan still . . .
Rome, in glades of peons, ruins,

Alexandrine and baroque, gilds
in the moon, and undone, irreligious
slums, where everything is unknown

that is not sex, caves inhabited
by faeces and children; the river-streets
from the Pincian to the Aventine,

to the slopes of the naked San Paolo
where the lights yellow the hot atmosphere,
resound with footsteps that stain

the damp stones, and the Roman evening,
echoing them, like a membrane scratched
by a vicious finger, reveals, more sharp,

the smell of urine.

VI

An army encamped and waiting
to become Christian in the Christian
city occupies a rotting expanse

of filthy grass in the burnt campagna:
he, too, hopes to go down amid
the civilian light, awaiting a human

abitazione, esso, sardo o pugliese,
dentro un porcile il fangoso desco
in villaggi ciechi tra lucide chiese

novecentesche e grattacieli.

Sotto le sue palpebre chiuse questo
assedio di milioni d'anime
dai crani ingenui, dall'occhio lesto

all'intesa, tra le infette marane
della borgata.

VII

Si perde verso il bianco Meridione,
azzurro, rosso, l'Appennino, assorto
sotto le chiuse palpebre, all'alone

del mare di Gaeta e di Sperlonga...
Dietro il Massico stende Sparanise
candelabri di ulivi, tra festoni
di piante rampicanti sulle elisie

radure, dove lucono i lampioni
a San Nicola... Si spalanca il golfo
affricano di Napoli, nazione

nel ventre della nazione...

E non più Jacopo (più recente è il sonno
di Ilaria) sotto le palpebre fonde
in civile forma il popolare mondo

italiano, e contro gli sfondi
del suo paesaggio, non più scarnisce
in luce di intelletto — che non nasconde

la buia materia — una mano che unisce
a Dio il povero rione. Quaggiù
tutto è preumano, e umanamente gioisce,

contro il riso del volgare fu

habitation, he from Puglia or Sardegna,
in a pigsty, the muddy slaughter-block
in blind villages with shining churches,

modern with skyscrapers.

Under his closed eyelids this
disheartened siege of a million souls
with naïve skulls, eyes quick

to catch on, among the infested swamps
of Pietralata.

VII

The Apennine, red, blue is lost along
the white South, absorbed under
the closed eyelids, in the halo

of the sea at Gaeta and Sperlonga . . .

Beyond Mount Massico, Sparanise
sets candelabra of olive-trees, in festoons
of plants climbing on the Elysian

glades, where the lamps shine
at San Nicola . . . the African bay
is thrown open at Naples, a nation

in the nation's belly . . .

And Jacopo no longer (more recent
is Ilaria's sleep) beneath that eyelid
sets in civil form the people's world

of Italy, and against the dry backgrounds
of his landscape no longer strips
in moral light, that does not hide

the body's darkness, a hand that unites
to God the poor neighborhood; down here
all is pre-human, and humanly rejoices,

against this vulgar laughter was

ed è inutile ogni parola
di redenzione: splende nella più

ardente indifferenza dei colori
seicenteschi, quasi che al sole
o all'ombra non bastasse che la sola

sfrontata presenza, di stracci, d'ori,
con negli occhi l'incallito riso
dei bassi digiuni d'amore.

Ragazzi romanzi sotto le palpebre
chiuse cantano nel cuore della specie
dei poveri rimasta sempre barbara

a tempi originari, esclusa alle vicende
segrete della luce cristiana,
al succedersi necessario dei secoli:

e fanno dell'Italia un loro possesso,
ironici, in un dialettale riso
che non città o provincia ma ossesso

poggio, rione, tiene in sè inciso,
se ognuno chiuso nel calore del sesso,
sua sola misura, vive tra una gente

abbandonata al cinismo più vero
e alla più vera passione; al violento
negarsi e al violento darsi; nel mistero

chiara, perchè pura e corrotta...

Se ognuno sa, esperto, l'ingenuo linguaggio
dell'incredulità, della insolenza,
dell'ironia, nel dialetto più saggio

e vizioso, chiude nell'incoscienza
le palpebre, si perde in un popolo
il cui clamore non è che silenzio.

and is useless any word
of salvation; here shines the most

glowing indifference in colors
of late Renaissance, as if for sun
or shade there was needed only

this bold presence, of rags, gold,
with—in the eyes—the calloused laugh
of the tenements fasting from love;

Latin boys under her closed
eyelids sing in the hearts of the race
of the poor who have stayed barbarians

from their very origin, excluded
from the secret events of Christian light,
from the necessary movement of the centuries;

and of Italy they make, ironically,
their own belonging, in a dialect of laughter
that no city or province but a ridge's

obsession, a neighborhood, keeps engraved
in itself; if each closed in heat of sex
his only measure, lives among a people

abandoned to the truest cynicism and the truest
passion; to violent denial of himself
and violent self-bestowal; clear

in its mystery, pure and corrupt . . .

If each, an expert, knows the naïve language
of incredulity, of insolence,
irony, in the wisest of dialects

and most vicious, he shuts his eyelids
without conscience, and is lost in a people
whose clamor is nothing but silence.

MARGHERITA GUIDACCI

Da « Giorno dei Santi »

Spesso ho pensato: è questa
La vera fine e Apocalisse dell'anno,
Col bruno e il grigio, due castoni vuoti,
Spente tutte le gemme dei colori
Che prima ci fissavano. Dissolto
È il mondo in questi fradici fermenti
Di morte. L'acqua porta
Via la terra dai monti finché resti
Nudo il macigno, il vento porta via
Le foglie fino all'ultima secchezza
Degli alberi. Non resta che sperare
Il tempo in cui piú nulla vi sarà
Da perdere. E già sotto
L'angoscia della carne si profila
Lo scheletro e riafferma la severa
Paziente attesa.
      È questa
La fine, non Dicembre coi suoi cieli
Di cristallo, la stella dell'Oriente
E gli uomini in ginocchio ad adorare
Il Fanciullo. In silenzio rivivrà
Anche se occulta al mondo la speranza
Col seme sotto la neve.
      Ma due volte
In questi giorni in cui la terra stessa
Assomiglia a una scena del Giudizio

Translated by Carlo L. Golino

From "All Saints' Day"

Often I have thought: is this
The year's true end, true Apocalypse,
In brown and grey, two empty settings,
Are all the precious stones devoid of colors
That earlier gazed at us. The world
In these decaying ferments of death
Is dissolved. The water carries
Away the soil from the mountains until
The rock is barren, the wind carries away
The leaves until the trees' last
Nakedness. All we can hope for
Is the time when nothing more
Is to be lost. Already under
The anguish of the flesh appears
The skeleton confirming the patient
Stern wait.
                        This is
The end, not December with its crystal
Skies, the star of the East
And kneeling men in worship
Of the Child. In silence, hope
Will live again even though hidden
With the seed under the snow.
                            But twice
In these days in which the very earth
Resembles a scene from the Judgment Day

A noi vien ricordato dall'altare
Colui che tornerà: non piú fanciullo
Per salvarci, ma adulto a giudicare
I vivi e i morti, a escludere ogni nuova
Redenzione. Si volgeranno allora
Squallidi e immensi i cardini del tempo
E l'eterno sarà. Voi solamente,
Santi, potrete osare di fissarlo.

* * *

Molte volte Novembre è ritornato
Nella mia vita, e questo che oggi ha inizio
Non è il peggiore: quieto
Benché non privo di apprensione. China
Mi trova su una culla, dove l'ultima
Mia nata dorme il misterioso
Profondo sonno dell'infanzia, ancora
Ospite piú che cittadina in questo
Nostro mondo per lei straniero. Sento
La dolce ondata del latte salirmi
Al seno: tenerezza
Che di sé gonfia tutte le mie fibre,
Dilata i miei confini. Qui lo stanco
Sangue si rifà puro a una segreta
Sorgente, si rifà vergine e può
Calmar la sete di vergini labbra.
Il mio corpo è strumento di miracolo
Come già fu nel dare vita. Il seno
È la collina favolosa, scorrono
I fiumi d'abbondanza in un'età
D'oro che segnerà
Per la creatura ignara il piú profondo
Alveo della memoria, a cui piú tardi
Ritornerà nel sogno o nel dolore...
Per lei intatta è l'immagine, per me
Che ne sono occasione, la scolora
Già il tempo, amaramente. È forse l'ultima
Volta che ho un figlio al seno, poiché incalzano

We are reminded from every altar
Of Him who shall return: no longer child
To save us, but grown man to judge
The living and the dead, to avert any new
Redemption. Then dreary and immense
Time's hinges will turn
And eternity will be. Only you,
O Saints, will dare behold it.

* * *

Many times November has returned
Into my life, the one upon this day beginning
Is not the worst; a quiet day
Though somewhat uneasy. It finds me
Bending over the cradle, where
My last-born sleeps an infant's
Deep, mysterious sleep, as yet a guest
Rather than citizen of this,
Our world, still strange to her. I feel
The sweet fullness of the milk rising
In my breast: a tenderness
That fills my every fiber,
Stretching my boundaries. Here the weary
Blood again turns pure at a secret
Spring, turning virginal it can
Quench the thirst of virgin lips.
My body is the instrument of miracle
As it was in giving life. The breast
Is the fabulous hill, rivers
Of abundance flow in a golden
Age that will mark
For the unknowing child her memory's
Deepest river bed, to which she
Will return later in dreams or sorrow . . .
For her the image is intact, for me,
Who am the occasion, time already
Bitterly discolors it. This is perhaps
The last time I shall nurse a child, since

Gli anni ad inaridire
La mia linfa. Oggi sono
Ancora un vivo albero, frusciante
Di foglie, benedetto
Di succhi, ma in cammino è la stagione
Spoglia che su di me si chiuderà.
Tanto piú dolce è questa sosta, prima
Ch'io stessa sia l'autunno: pure un'ombra
Di presagio la vela e di paura.
Il passato si stende alle mie spalle
Come una lunga via. So del futuro
Solo una cosa: che difficilmente
Potrà uguagliare per me la durata
Del tempo ch'è trascorso.

The pressing years are drying up
My vital lymph. Today I am
Still a tree alive, rustling
With leaves, blessed
With sap, but the barren season advances
That will close upon me.
So much sweeter is this pause, then, before
I, myself, become the autumn; still a hazy
Omen and fear veil it.
The past stretches out behind my back
Like a long road. Of the future
I know only one thing: for me,
Its duration will hardly equal
That of the time gone by.

NOTES ON THE POETS

BARTOLINI, LUIGI (1892——)
Born in Cupramontana (Ancona). Poet, writer, painter, etcher, but in every field a highly individualistic and tormented artist. Began writing when very young. His independent character brought him into trouble with the Fascist government, and he was sent to the "confino" for several months in 1933. Now lives in Rome.
Poetical works: *Il guanciale* (Turin: Gobetti, 1924); *Poesie* (Rome: Modernissima, 1939); *Poesie ad Anna Stikler* (Venice: Il Cavallino, 1941); *Poesie e Satire* (Rome: Documento, 1944); *Liriche e polemiche* (Pisa: Nistri-Lischi, 1948); *Pianete* (Florence: Vallechi, 1953); *Ombra fra le metope* (Milan: Schwarz, 1953); *Poesie per Anita e Luciana* (Milan: Scheiwiller, 1953); *Addio ai sogni* (Milan: Scheiwiller, 1954); *Al padre ed altri versi* (Milan: Miano, 1959); *Poesie 1960* (Ancona: Bucciarelli, 1960).
The poems in this anthology were taken from *Pianete*.

BERTOLUCCI, ATTILIO (1911——)
Born in San Lazzaro (Parma). Lived in Parma until 1952 when he moved to Rome. Has taught history of art and has been an art critic for many years. Edits the review *Paragone*.
Poetical works: *Sirio* (Parma: Minardi, 1929); *Fuochi in novembre* (Parma: Minardi, 1934); *La capanna indiana* (Florence: Sansoni, 1950, 1955).
The poems in this anthology were taken from *La capanna indiana* (Florence: Sansoni, 1955).

BETOCCHI, CARLO (1899——)
Born in Turin. Studied in Florence, where he was graduated as a land surveyor. Served in the First World War and since then has lived in Florence, Bologna, Rome, and in many parts of northern Italy. Now teaches in Florence.
Poetical works: *Realtà vince il sogno* (Florence: Frontespizio, 1932); *Altre poesie* (Florence: Vallecchi, 1939); *Notizie di prosa e poesia*

(Florence: Vallecchi, 1947); *Un ponte nella pianura* (Milan: Schwarz, 1953); *Poesie* (Florence: Vallecchi, 1955).

The poems in this anthology were taken from *Poesie* (Florence: Vallecchi, 1955).

CAMPANA, DINO (1885–1932)

Born in Marradi (Tuscany). After vain attempts at a formal education, he began roaming over Europe and South America. Even in his youth he showed signs of mental instability, which became almost a permanent illness as he grew older. Was in mental hospitals several times in Italy and in other countries. Was jailed once in Switzerland and once in Italy. Worked as a knife-sharpener, as a fireman, in the Argentine pampas, aboard ships, as a doorman, and in many other occupations. He died in the psychiatric hospital of Castel Pulci. Campana has been a fundamental influence on the development of Italian poetry.

Poetical works: *Canti Orfici* (Marradi: Ravagli, 1941. 2d and 3d eds.; Florence: Vallecchi, 1928, 1942); *Inediti* (Florence: Vallecchi, 1942); *Canti Orfici e altri scritti* (Florence: Vallechi, 1952). The poems in this anthology were taken from *Canti Orfici e altri scritti* (Florence: Vallechi, 1952).

CARDARELLI, VINCENZO (pseudonym of NAZARENO CALDARELLI) (1887–1960)

Born in Corneto Tarquinia (Rome). Moved to Rome in his teens and after trying many trades he became a journalist. In 1911 he moved to Florence, and in 1919 he returned to Rome where in the same year he founded the review *La Ronda*, one of the most important Italian magazines in the period immediately following the First World War. From 1949 to the time of his death he directed the weekly *La Fiera Letteraria*.

Poetical works: *Prologhi* (Milan: S.E.L., 1916); *Il sole a picco* (Bologna: l'Italiano, 1928. 2d ed.; Milan: Mondadori, 1952); *Prologhi, viaggi e favole* (Lanciano: Carabba, 1929. 2d ed.; Milan: Mondadori, 1946); *Giorni in piena* (Rome: Novissima, 1936); *Poesie* (Rome: Novissima, 1936. 2d ed.; Milan: Mondadori, 1943. Six further eds. by Mondadori).

The poems in this anthology were taken from *Poesie* (Milan: Mondadori, 1955).

CORAZZINI, SERGIO (1886–1907)

Born in Rome. Had to leave school because of family financial difficulties. Became ill with tuberculosis and at the beginning of 1907 was placed in a sanatorium in Nettuno. He died a few months later in Rome.

Poetical works: all the poems of Corazzini have been collected in *Liriche* (Milan-Naples: Riccardo Ricciardi, 1922, 1959).

The poems in this anthology have been taken from *Liriche* (Milan-Naples: Riccardo Ricciardi, 1959).

DE LIBERO, LIBERO (1906———)

Born in Fondi in the Ciociaria region between Rome and Naples. Moved to Rome in his early twenties to continue his studies, but became instead a writer and a journalist. De Libero's poetry seems to find its inspiration in his native land, which he depicts with a deep affection.

Poetical works: *Il libro del forestiere-Poesie 1930–1942* (Rome: Nuove Edizioni Italiane, 1945. 2d ed.; Milan: Mondadori, 1946); *Banchetto-Poesie 1943–1947* (Milan: Mondadori, 1949); *Ascolta la Ciociaria* (Rome: De Luca, 1953. 2d ed.; Milan: Scheiwiller, 1953).

The poem in this anthology was taken from *Banchetto* (Milan: Mondadori, 1949).

GATTO, ALFONSO (1909———)

Born in Salerno. Never completed his studies although he attended the university for three years. Began his career as a journalist and as an art critic. In 1938 with Vasco Pratolini he edited the review *Campo di Marte*. Now lives in Florence, and after a short interlude as a teacher, he is again a journalist.

Poetical works: *Isola* (Naples: Libreria del '900, 1932); *Morto ai paesi* (Modena: Guanda, 1937); *Poesie* (Milan: Panorama, 1939. 2d ed.; Florence: Vallecchi, 1941); *Amore della vita* (Milan: Rosa and Ballo, 1944); *Il capo sulla neve* (Milan: Milano-Sera, 1946); *Nuove poesie* (Milan: Mondadori, 1950); *La forza degli occhi* (Milan: Mondadori, 1954).

The poems in this anthology were taken from *Isola* ("Erba e latte") and from *Morto ai paesi* ("Morto ai paesi," "Piangerà chi non piange").

GOVONI, CORRADO (1884———)

Born in Tàmara (Ferrara). Published his first verses at the age of twenty. Was strongly influenced by the crepuscolari and particularly by Corazzini, who became his close friend. Also participated in the futurist movement in Milan, where he then resided. Since 1928 he has lived in Rome, where he still actively practices his profession of writer.

Poetical works: *Le fiale* (Florence: Lumachi, 1903. 2d ed.; Milan: Garzanti, 1949); *Armonia in grigio et in silentio* (Florence: Lumachi, 1903); *Fuochi d'artificio* (Palermo: Ganguzza-Lajosa, 1905); *Gli aborti* (Ferrara: Taddei, 1907); *Poesie elettriche* (Milan: Poesia, 1911. 2d ed.; Ferrara: Taddei, 1919); *Inaugurazione della primavera* (Florence: La

Voce, 1915. 2d ed.; Ferrara: Taddei, 1919); *Rarefazioni* (Milan: Poesia, 1915); *Poesie scelte* (Ferrara: Taddei, 1919); *Quaderno dei sogni e delle stelle* (Milan: Mondadori, 1924); *Brindisi alla notte* (Milan: Poesia, 1924); *Il flauto magico* (Rome: Al tempo della fortuna, 1932); *Canzoni a bocca chiusa* (Florence: Vallecchi, 1938); *Pellegrino d'amore* (Milan: Mondadori, 1941); *Govonigiotto* (Milan: S.T.E.L.I., 1943); *Aladino* (Milan: Mondadori, 1946); *L'Italia odia i poeti* (Rome: Pagine Nuove, 1950); *Patria d'alto volo* (Siena: Maia, 1953); *Preghiera al trifoglio* (Rome: Casini, 1953): *Manoscritto nella bottiglia* (Milan: Mondadori, 1954); *Stradario della primavera* (Venice: Neri Pozza, 1958).

The poems in this anthology were taken from *Poesie scelte* (Ferrara: Taddei, 1919).

Gozzano, Guido (1883–1916)

Born in Turin. Began to write when very young, publishing his poetry in various magazines and newspapers with unusual success. Made several trips to various parts of the world in an abortive search for a benign climate that would relieve his chronic tuberculosis. He died in Italy.

Poetical works: all the poems of Gozzano have been collected in *Le poesie di Gozzano* (Milan: Garzanti, 1960), and the poems in this anthology have been taken from this volume.

Guidacci, Margherita (1921——)

Born in Florence. Attended the university of her native city and was graduated in English literature in 1943. Married the writer Luca Prima in 1949; three children. Now lives and teaches in Rome.

Poetical works: *La sabbia e l'angelo* (Florence: Vallecchi, 1946); *Morte del ricco* (Florence: Vallecchi, 1955); *Il giorno dei Santi* (Milan: Scheiwiller, 1957).

The poems in this anthology were taken from *Il giorno dei Santi* (Milan: Scheiwiller, 1957).

Jahier, Piero (1884——)

Born in Genoa. Began his literary career with the *Voce* group. Spent three years at the front in the First World War. Under fascism he lived in Bologna as an employee of the state railroads and was closely watched by the police because of his political ideas. He is now retired in Florence.

Poetical works: *Ragazzo* (Rome: La Voce, 1919); *Con me e con gli Alpini* (Florence: La Voce, 1919. 2d ed.; Turin: Einaudi, 1943); *Ragazzo e prime poesie* (Florence: Vallecchi, 1939).

The poem in this anthology was taken from *Ragazzo e prime poesie* (Florence: Vallecchi, 1939).

Luzi, Mario (1914——)
Born in Florence, where he still lives and teaches. Was one of the first contributors to *Campo di Marte* and *Letteratura*. He is usually considered to be the most significant poet among the younger hermetics.
Poetical works: *La barca* (Modena: Guanda, 1935. 2d ed.; Florence: Parenti, 1942); *Avvento Notturno* (Florence: Vallecchi, 1940); *Un brindisi* (Florence: Sansoni, 1946); *Quaderno Gotico* (Florence: Vallecchi, 1946); *Primizie del deserto* (Milan: Schwarz, 1952); *Onore del vero* (Venice: Neri Pozza, 1957); *Il giusto della vita* (Milan: Garzanti, 1960).
The poems in this anthology were taken from *Un brindisi* (Florence: Sansoni, 1946).

Montale, Eugenio (1896——)
Born in Genoa. Mostly self-educated. Served as an infantry officer during the First World War. In 1922 in Turin he, together with other writers, founded the review *Primo Tempo*. The review was short-lived but was highly significant during its brief life. In 1927 he moved to Florence as director of the Gabinetto Vieusseux. Since 1947 he has been editor of the Milanese daily *Il Corriere della Sera*. Besides being a poet, Montale has been very active as a literary critic and as a translator. He is usually considered to be one of the three greatest living poets of Italy along with Ungaretti and Quasimodo.
Poetical works: *Ossi di seppia* (Turin: Gobetti, 1925. 2d ed.; Turin: Ribet, 1928. 3d ed.; Lanciano: Carabba, 1931. 4th ed.; Turin: Einaudi, 1942); *La casa dei doganieri e altre poesie* (Florence: Antico Fattore, 1932); *Le occasioni* (Turin: Einaudi, 1930); *Finisterre* (Lugano: Quaderni di Lugano, 1943. 2d ed.; Florence: Barbera, 1945); *La bufera ed altro* (Venice: Neri Pozza, 1957). The complete works of Montale are now being republished by Mondadori of Milan.
The poems in this anthology were taken from *Ossi di seppia* ("Falsetto") (Milan: Mondadori, 1955), from *La bufera ed altro* ("L'arca," "Giorno e notte," "L'anguilla") (Milan: Mondadori, 1956), and the others from *Le occasioni* (Milan: Mondadori, 1957).

Palazzeschi, Aldo (pseudonym of Aldo Giurlani (1885——)
Born in Florence. Published his first verses at his own expense. An active supporter of the futurist movement in its initial phase. Before the First World War he wrote for many avant-garde reviews, particularly *La Voce*. Then moved to Rome and devoted himself exclusively to the writing of novels and short stories.
Poetical works: *I cavalli bianchi* (Florence, 1905); *Lanterna* (Florence, 1907); *Poemi* (Florence, 1908); *L'incendiario* (Milan: Poesia, 1910);

Poesie (1904–1910) (Florence: Vallecchi, 1925. Definitive ed.; Milan: Preda, 1930); *Difetti 1905* (Milan: Garzanti, 1947); *Viaggio sentimentale* (Milan: Scheiwiller, 1955); *Opere giovanili* (Milan: Mondadori, 1959).

The poems in this anthology were taken from *Poesie* (Florence: Vallecchi, 1925).

PAPINI, GIOVANNI (1881–1956)

Born in Florence. Papini occupies a special position in the cultural and intellectual history of Italy in this century. From his first to his latest writings he has always given evidence of a singular polemical and critical spirit, often destructive in appearance, but actually always inspired by the desire for improvement and progress. In 1903 with G. Prezzolini he founded the *Leonardo*. A few years later he was the editor of *Il Regno*. Was one of the founders of *La Voce* and soon after joined the futurist movement with the review *Lacerba*. Shortly after the First World War he became reconverted to Catholicism and thereafter his works always had a strong religious inspiration. Poet, critic, novelist, short-story writer, editor—Papini was throughout his life a powerful and moving force in Italian culture.

Poetical works: *Poesia in versi* (Florence: Vallecchi, 1932), which includes also *Opera prima 1914–1916* and *Pane e vino 1921–1926*.

The poem in this anthology was taken from *Poesia in versi*.

PASOLINI, PIER PAOLO (1922——)

Born in Bologna. One of the youngest and most controversial writers of modern Italy. After a brief attempt at teaching he now lives exclusively from his writings and from his work in the film industry as a scriptwriter and as an actor.

Poetical works: *I diarii* (Casarsa: Pubblicazioni dell'Academiuta, 1945); *Dal Diario (1945–1947)* (Caltanisetta: Sciascia, 1954); *Il canto popolare* (Milan: Meridiana, 1954); *Le ceneri di Gramsci* (Milan: Garzanti, 1957); *L'usignolo della Chiesa Cattolica (1943–1949)* (Milan: Longanesi, 1958); *Sonetto primaverile* (Milan: Scheiwiller, 1960).

The poem in this anthology was taken from *Le ceneri di Gramsci* (Milan: Garzanti, 1957).

PAVESE, CESARE (1908–1950)

Born in Santo Stefano Belbo (Turin). For many years he taught, but his greatest activity was as a translator, especially from American authors. No other man did as much as Pavese did in the early thirties to introduce American literature to Italy. His translation of *Moby Dick* is a masterpiece of its kind. Because of his political activity he was jailed and "confined" several times by the Fascist police. After the war when the struggle seemed over, he committed suicide.

Poetical works: *Lavorare stanca* (Florence: Solaria, 1936, 2d ed.; Turin: Einaudi, 1943); *Verrà la morte e avrà i tuoi occhi* (Turin: Einaudi, 1951).

The poems in this anthology were taken from *Lavorare stanca* ("Estate") (Turin: Einaudi, 1943) and from *Verrà la morte e avrà i tuoi occhi* ("La terra e la morte") (Turin: Einaudi, 1951).

PENNA, SANDRO (1906——)

Born in Perugia. Lives in Rome, where he has no particular profession except that of poet. To supplement his income from poetry he occasionally resorts to varied occupations.

Poetical works: *Poesie* (Florence: Parenti, 1938); *Appunti* (Milan: La Meridiana, 1950); *Una strana gioia di vivere* (Milan: Scheiwiller, 1956); *Poesie* (Milan: Garzanti, 1957); *Croce e delizia* (Milan: Longanesi, 1958).

The poems in this anthology were taken from *Poesie* (Milan: Garzanti, 1957).

QUASIMODO, SALVATORE (1901——)

Born in Syracuse (Sicily). Because of the many hardships of his early life, Quasimodo's education was very haphazard. In his twenties he traveled over most of Italy as an employee of the State Civil Engineers Bureau. In the early thirties he moved to Milan and he still resides there. His first poems appeared in *Solaria* in 1930, and since then he has contributed to the principal reviews of Italy. In 1959 he was awarded the Nobel Prize for Literature.

Poetical works: *Acque e terre* (Florence: Solaria, 1930); *Óboe sommerso* (Genoa: Circoli, 1932); *Odore di eucalyptus e altri versi* (Florence: Antico Fattore, 1933); *Erato e Apollion* (Milan: Scheiwiller, 1936); *Poesie* (Milan: Primi Piani, 1938); *Ed è subito sera* (Milan: Mondadori, 1942); *Con il piede straniero sopra il cuore* (Milan: Costume, 1946); *Giorno dopo giorno* (Milan: Mondadori, 1947); *La vita non è sogno* (Milan: Mondadori, 1949); *Il falso e vero verde* (Milan: Mondadori, 1956); *La terra impareggiabile* (Milan: Mondadori, 1958); *The Selected Writings of Salvatore Quasimodo* (New York: Farrar, Straus & Cudahy, 1960).

The poems and translations in this anthology were taken from *The Selected Writings of Salvatore Quasimodo*, copyright 1954, 1960 by Arnoldo Mondadori Editore; used by permission of the publishers, Farrar, Straus & Cudahy, Inc.

RÈBORA, CLEMENTE (1885–1957)

Born in Milan. Rèbora is perhaps the most important poet of modern Italy who found his inspiration in a deep, almost mystical religious faith. After a brief attempt at teaching he joined the Italian army in the

First World War. After a long period at the front he was wounded in an explosion. He remained in hospital for several months and although he recovered he was afflicted by nervous disorders for many years. After the war he devoted himself completely to his literary work, leading a very retired life. He was deeply agitated by spiritual problems and in 1931 he moved to a convent. In 1936 he was ordained a priest.

Poetical works: *Frammenti lirici* (Florence: La Voce, 1913); *Canti anonimi* (Milan: Il Convegno Editoriale, 1922); *Le poesie (1913–1947)* (Florence: Vallecchi, 1947); *Canti dell'infermità* (Milan: Scheiwiller, 1957).

The poems in this anthology were taken from *Canti anonimi*.

Saba, Umberto (1883–1957)

Born in Trieste. Although widely regarded as one of the more important Italian poets of this century, Saba never really participated in the intellectual life of the country. In his native city, which was not reunited with Italy until 1918, he remained at the periphery of Italian letters and out of the prevailing currents. His poetry is highly individualistic and remarkably different from the general pattern.

Poetical works: *Poesie* (Florence: Casa Editrice Italiana, 1911); *Coi miei occhi* (Florence: La Voce, 1912); *Cose leggere e vaganti* (Trieste: Libreria Antica e Moderna, 1920); *Canzoniere* (Trieste: Libreria Antica e Moderna, 1921); *Preludio e Canzonette* (Turin: Primo Tempo, 1922); *Autobiografia, I prigioni* (Turin: Primo Tempo, 1924); *Figure e Canti* (Milan: Treves, 1928); *Tre composizioni* (Milan: Treves, 1933); *Ammonizioni e altre poesie* (Trieste: by the author, 1933); *Parole* (Lanciano: Carabba, 1934); *Ultime cose* (Lugano, 1944); *Il Canzoniere* (Turin: Einaudi, 1945); *Mediterranee* (Milan: Mondadori, 1946); *Uccelli* (Trieste: Zibaldone, 1950); *Il Canzoniere* (Milan: Garzanti, 1951); *Quasi un racconto* (Milan: Mondadori, 1951). The complete works of Saba are now being republished by Mondadori of Milan.

The poems in this anthology were taken from *Il Canzoniere* (Turin: Einaudi, 1945).

Sbarbaro, Camillo (1888——)

Born in Santa Margherita Ligure on the Italian Riviera. Published his first collection of verses in 1911 with funds raised by admiring schoolmates. Lived most of his life in Genoa, where he taught Greek. Since his retirement a few years ago he has been living at Spotorno on the western Italian Riviera.

Poetical works: *Resine* (Genoa: Caimo, 1911. 2d ed.; Milan: Garzanti, 1948); *Pianissimo* (Florence: La Voce, 1914. 2d ed.; Venice: Neri Pozza, 1954); *Rimanenze* (Milan: Scheiwiller, 1955); *Primizie* (Milan: Scheiwiller, 1958).

The poem in this anthology was taken from *Pianissimo*.

SERENI, VITTORIO (1913――)
Born in Luino (Varese). Lives in Milan, where he is employed by the publishing house of Mondadori. Before and after the last war, he had taught in Milan. Was a prisoner of war in North Africa in the Second World War.

Poetical works: *Frontiera* (Milan: Corrente, 1941); *Poesie* (Florence: Vallecchi, 1942); *Diario d'Algeria* (Florence: Vallecchi, 1947).

The poems in this anthology were taken from *Diario d'Algeria* ("Ma se tu manchi") and from *Poesie*.

UNGARETTI, GIUSEPPE (1888――)
Born in Alexandria (Egypt) of Italian parents. Studied in Paris at the Sorbonne and came to Italy just before the First World War. During the war he served in the Italian army both in Italy and in France. In 1920 he moved to Rome, where he collaborated with *La Ronda* group. Then became a journalist and traveled widely in Europe. In 1936 he went to Brazil as professor of Italian literature at the University of São Paulo. Returned to Italy in 1943 and was appointed professor of modern Italian literature at the University of Rome.

Poetical works: *Il porto sepolto* (Udine: Stabilimento Tipografico Friulano, 1916); *Allegria di naufragi* (Florence: Vallecchi, 1919); *L'allegria* (Milan: Preda, 1931); *Sentimento del tempo* (Florence: Vallecchi, 1933); *Poesie disperse* (Milan: Mondadori, 1945); *Il dolore* (Milan: Mondadori, 1947); *La terra promessa* (Milan: Mondadori, 1950); *Un grido e paesaggi* (Milan: Schwarz, 1952); *Vita di un uomo* (Milan: Mondadori, 1958–1960), which includes the complete works of Ungaretti; *Life of a Man* (London: Hamilton; New York: New Directions; Milan: Scheiwiller, 1958).

The poems in this anthology were taken from *Vita di un uomo* (Milan: Mondadori, 1958).

www.ingramcontent.com/pod-product-compliance
Lightning Source LLC
Chambersburg PA
CBHW021702230426
43668CB00008B/699